More Praise for *Bulle*

"This manual takes spiritual warfare seriously by [...] Savior's eyes at our enemies as well as at ourselve[...]

—Louie Crew, founder, Integrity

"Candace Chellew-Hodge knows that you can be lesbian and Christian. This book will help every person who is both gay and Christian to have that same confidence. It will also enable heterosexual allies to better understand how their gay friends feel and it may shake those who assume that gay and Christian cannot go together. The Spiritual survival exercises move the reader beyond just knowledge to life more abundant."

—Jack Rogers, professor of theology emeritus, San Francisco Theological Seminary, and author of *Jesus, the Bible, and Homosexuality*

"*Bulletproof Faith*, though written for the gay and lesbian community, is a primer in developing an authentic and examined faith. Candace Chellew-Hodge suggests there is no faith more powerful than the faith of gay and lesbian Christians. In reading this book, I am convinced and humbled."

—James Mulholland, pastor and coauthor, *If God Is Love* and *If Grace Is True*

"Reading Candace Chellew-Hodge's book, *Bulletproof Faith*, is just as enriching as meeting her in person. Candace takes the most controversial issue of our day, puts a human face on it, and calls us to love as fully and graciously as Jesus did. I commend this book to all who've struggled with human sexuality, which is to say, all of us."

—Philip Gulley, Quaker writer, pastor, and co-author, *If God Is Love* and *If Grace Is True*

"In *Bulletproof Faith* we learn why Candace Chellew-Hodge has been such an effective advocate for lesbian, gay, bisexual, and transgender people for so many years. Her faith encourages and empowers her even as it disarms her opponents. And here's more good news—your faith can do the same!"

—Harry Knox, director, Human Rights Campaign Foundation's Religion and Faith Program

BULLETPROOF
FAI†H

A **SPIRITUAL SURVIVAL GUIDE** FOR **GAY** AND **LESBIAN CHRISTIANS**

Candace Chellew-Hodge

JOSSEY-BASS
A Wiley Imprint
www.josseybass.com

Published by Jossey-Bass
A Wiley Imprint
989 Market Street, San Francisco, CA 94103-1741—www.josseybass.com

Jossey-Bass books and products are available through most bookstores. To contact Jossey-Bass directly call our Customer Care Department within the U.S. at 800-956-7739, outside the U.S. at 317-572-3986, or fax 317-572-4002.

Jossey-Bass also publishes its books in a variety of electronic formats. Some content that appears in print may not be available in electronic books.

Library of Congress Cataloging-in-Publication Data

Chellew-Hodge, Candace.
  Bulletproof faith : a spiritual survival guide for gay and lesbian Christians /
Candace Chellew-Hodge.
      p. cm.
  Includes bibliographical references.
  ISBN 978-0-470-27928-1 (cloth)
  1. Gays—Religious life. I. Title.
  BV4596.G38C44 2008
  248.8'408664—dc22

                                                      2008018499

Printed in the United States of America
FIRST EDITION
HB Printing   10 9 8 7 6 5 4 3 2 1

Contents

For Wanda,
my home

Acknowledgments

Truth be told, this book has been in the making for ten years now. It was 1998 when I first wrote about the idea of "spiritual self-defense" for gay, lesbian, bisexual, and transgender Christians. The workshop I developed around my writings was well received at every conference where it was presented. I knew there was a hunger for this kind of material within the GLBT community. I am grateful to everyone who attended those workshops and provided the valuable feedback that came to be incorporated into this book.

I am especially grateful to Steve Schwartz, my agent at the Sarah Jane Freymann Literary Agency. He did what I was told no agent would do—he gave me valuable advice and guidance that helped me improve this book even before he took me on as a client. I am thankful for his generosity and diligence.

Many thanks to my editor, Sheryl Fullerton, who talked me down from the literary ledge and reminded me that it's not all about me. That's an accomplishment for any editor who has to deal with a writer's fragile ego. Thanks to Bruce Emmer, my copyeditor, for skillfully cleaning up my messy sentences without sacrificing my voice, and to Joanne Clapp Fullagar, my production manager, for her patient guidance and immediate enthusiasm for this book.

Thanks also to Mike Hughes, who gave me back early transcripts of the book bathed in red ink. As one of my best friends and best teachers, he taught me to speak and write in ways that reach the most ears and hearts. His friendship is both a joy and a challenge to me, and I know my life would be poorer without him.

I am grateful to all the spiritual leaders and teachers who have helped to shape my faith:

Reverend Paul Turner, the senior pastor at Gentle Spirit Christian Church in Atlanta, Georgia, who relished our theological jousting and never gave up on me even though I resisted his predictions that I would enter the ministry

Reverend Andy Sidden, the senior pastor at Garden of Grace United Church of Christ in Columbia, South Carolina (where I am privileged to serve as associate pastor), who has helped me become a better leader and minister

Nancy Beaver, my spiritual director, who without fail puts me back in touch with God whenever I lose my way

To all my "enemies" who condemn me, argue with me, and challenge me to delve deeper into my relationship with God and work to develop a bulletproof faith I say, this book would have been impossible without you.

I am most grateful to my beloved partner, Wanda. She has always stood beside me and encouraged me to pursue my dreams, no matter how crazy they may seem to her. She is the most grace-filled, most generous, and kindest person I know, and one day I hope to be half the Christian she is. She has taught me what it is like to embody Christ in this world. Her faith is truly bulletproof.

C.C.H.

Introduction:
There Is Only One Side

She is not the other side of the issue!

That's all I could think while the television cameraman put a wireless microphone on the woman, preparing to interview her.

She is not the other side of the issue!

The woman had approached our group, about twenty of us, as we held a silent vigil outside a concert hall in Columbia, South Carolina. She began to yell at us, wagging her finger, one hand on her hip.

"God hates you!" she cried at the top of her lungs. "Whoever told you God loves you was wrong. That's a lie from the pit of hell!"

We were holding our vigil to protest the inclusion of an antigay gospel singer at a fundraising concert for Democratic presidential candidate Barack Obama in September 2007. We were vastly outnumbered by the hundreds of concertgoers and Obama supporters who crowded around the theater entrance on the other side of the road. We had largely been ignored or simply stared at by those waiting for the doors to open. But we were this woman's personal crusade.

"God made man and *wo*-man!" she proclaimed, leaning into her scolding like the mother of an unruly child.

News organizations from around the country were there to cover the controversy, and one by one, they clipped a microphone to this woman and rolled tape. She refused to give her name but was proud to spout her venom for the cameras.

When a reporter finally asked me my opinion, I tried to explain that this woman did not represent the other side of the issue. The reporter wanted to know why.

"Because there is no other side to this issue."

For years, the media have attempted to "balance" the "homosexual issue" with voices from the "other side." That "other side" has traditionally been voices from religion, specifically the Christian religion. I'm not quite sure how religious voices got to be the "other side" of this issue other than that is the side that has screamed the loudest against the full inclusion of gay, lesbian, bisexual, and transgender (GLBT) people in church and society. Since that's the only voice of opposition that has been raised, the media reason that it must then be the "other side" of the issue. What has resulted has been the false dichotomy of "gays versus God." The media perpetuate the myth that either you're gay, lesbian, bisexual, or transgender or you're *religious*, and never the twain shall meet. If they do, it's the GLBT *religious* person that is suspect—or made to be an oddity—and not the non-GLBT religious person.

Religion is not the "other side" of the "homosexual issue" any more than people who believe in a flat earth are the "other side" of the global warming issue or any more than the Ku Klux Klan is the "other side" of the black civil rights movement. Despite the media's relentless search for the "other side," for some issues, there simply isn't a viable "other side." This issue is one of them.

If there really were an authentic "other side" to this issue, it would come from science. Alfred Kinsey, in 1948, theorized that sexual orientation is more fluid and more nuanced than simply heterosexual or homosexual.[1] His research produced the Kinsey Scale, which traced sexuality on a continuum. Most people fall somewhere between exclusively heterosexual and exclusively homosexual. More recent research has produced strong evidence that sexual orientation (and often gender identity) has some biological roots.[2] The issue of environmental influence is yet to be resolved, but science seems to be bearing out that GLBT people are "that way" because they were created "that way." Mounting evidence convinced the American Psychological Association to remove homosexuality from its list of mental disorders in 1973. Scientists now understand that sexual orientation is not a religious issue but a biological issue that should be studied in a neutral and scientific manner—not through the lens of morality.

That's not to say, of course, that being born gay, lesbian, bisexual, or transgender automatically confers morality. Heterosexuality is presumed to be an inborn trait, yet that, in and of itself, does not make a person moral. Some inborn traits are certainly harmful, such as a biological leaning toward addiction, disease, or mental illness. Sexual orientation itself, however—be it heterosexual, homosexual, or somewhere in between on the spectrum—is neither a moral issue nor harmful in and of itself. A person's innate sexual orientation is irrelevant to concepts of morality.

The question of morality intersects with sexual orientation only in consideration of how we use our sexuality. The scriptures can be a valid guide here, but arguments regarding morality must apply to persons of all sexual orientations. The scriptures address sexual immorality in three main categories: adultery, prostitution, and rape. Adultery breaks a covenant of commitment between partners, prostitution is the practice of using another person for sexual gratification, and rape is the abuse of another in a sexual manner. Eugene Peterson captures it perfectly in his translation of 1 Corinthians 6:9 (a passage frequently used to condemn GLBT people) in *The Message*: "Don't you realize that this is not the way to live? Unjust people who don't care about God will not be joining in his kingdom. Those who use and abuse each other, use and abuse sex, use and abuse the earth and everything in it, don't qualify as citizens in God's kingdom."

Nevertheless, the Bible contains numerous accounts of people who behave immorally whose acts are not condemned: King David commits adultery with Bathsheba (2 Samuel 11:2–5) but is still identified as a man after God's own heart (1 Samuel 13:14). Lot offers his daughters to be raped by the population of Sodom in Genesis 19 but is still counted as a righteous man by God (2 Peter 2:7). In Judges 19:14–29, a Levite visiting Gibeah is taken in by a farmer. Men appear at the farmer's door threatening to attack the Levite. Instead, the farmer's virgin daughter and the Levite's concubine are offered to the crowd, which takes the concubine and rapes her all night long. She dies from the attack. Yet none of these instances of heterosexual immorality is used to condemn heterosexuality per se.

Despite these passages of dubious morality, the Bible elsewhere condemns all forms of sexual abuse and the sexual violation of the covenant that exists between couples. Indeed, when the Bible speaks of relationships on all levels, the most blessed relationship is one of love: "If we love one another, God abides in us and God's love is perfected in us" (1 John 4:12).

Love is the measure of all relationships; no mention is made of sexual orientation or even gender. If love, commitment, and fidelity are present, so is God, no matter what the configuration of the couple. Not one word in the Bible condemns loving, committed relationships. God calls us all, not just heterosexuals, to be moral in our sexuality—keeping our covenants and refusing to use or abuse anyone sexually. This is the only role religion plays in sexuality. It is a guide to responsible sexuality regardless of orientation.

Once we understand that there is no valid "other side" to the "homosexual issue," our faith can grow and become bulletproof. When we hear arguments against us based on Scripture, we know they hold no water—they have no power over us.

You hold in your hands a guide to becoming bulletproof. Like any worthwhile undertaking, becoming bulletproof takes time. Simply understanding, on an intellectual level, what makes one spiritually bulletproof is only half the battle. You can have all the knowledge you want, but that won't help you when emotions run high in an argument with friends or family. It's only when we develop the heart knowledge of God's unconditional and enduring love for us that we can become bulletproof—calm and assured even when emotions are high.

This book will guide you through the minefield of condemnation and persecution faced daily by GLBT Christians. Check out this book's Web site at http://www.bulletproofbook.com for a free study guide and other supplemental tools for becoming bulletproof. Some of you may object to the concept of becoming "bulletproof," arguing that the term is too violent or militaristic. However, I believe that the vitriol that stems from the deep homophobia[3] of our society demands such a severe title. To survive the dire attacks our community faces, you truly have to be bulletproof or you will die—if not physically, then at least spiritually.

Let's put it this way: What would it take for me to convince you to commit suicide? Let's say I harangued you daily. I called you on the phone, text-messaged you, and sent you e-mails every single day telling you how worthless you are, what a jerk you are, how the world would be a better place without you, and how much God hates people like you. Could I convince you to kill yourself? Probably not. Instead, you'd probably think I was a kook and would get a restraining order against me. One person telling you that you're worthless is simply a nuisance.

Now let's say the message that you are worthless and hated by God permeated the society where you lived. You receive this message daily from your family, your friends, your church, your society, and your government. Day after day, you are told that you are sick and sinful, an abomination before God, and doomed to eternal damnation. In addition, your government denies you basic civil rights. That kind of constant abuse from the world could, very easily, lead to thoughts of suicide. At the very least, it could lead you to give up on God and abandon your spirituality.

The effects of this kind of ongoing social and religious abuse are real. The U.S. government issued a report in 1989 showing that gay and lesbian youth are two to three times more likely to attempt suicide than other young people and may account for as many as 30 percent of completed youth suicides annually.[4] That research has been disputed and the numbers may be lower, but a 1991 University of Minnesota study of 150 gay and lesbian youths in Minneapolis revealed that more than 30 percent said they had attempted suicide at least once as a teenager.[5] What's not in dispute, however, is that stress, violence, lack of support, family problems, and substance abuse are prevalent in our community because society doesn't accept us or support us.

To face this kind of society, we need to be bulletproof. We must realize that our enemies are real and are working not just to deny us basic rights in society but to annihilate us altogether. Becoming bulletproof is really our only viable option, or the result may be suicide—physical or spiritual.

We're told in Ephesians 6:13–17 to put on "the whole armor of God." That armor includes righteousness, truth, peace, salvation, and Spirit. It's no coincidence that faith is our shield to "quench all the flaming arrows" that come our way. This is the ancient Christian equivalent of the bulletproof vest, and it had to be arrow- and spear-proof. Our modern-day shield of faith has to be strong enough to protect us from all attacks so that we emerge safe and secure. Without this shield of faith, we cannot survive as GLBT Christians in this world. As you venture into a world hostile to GLBT people, and especially GLBT people of faith, take this book as your guide, put on the whole armor of God, and become bulletproof.

BULLETPROOF
FAI†H

1

BECOMING BULLETPROOF

Always be prepared to make a defense to any one
who calls you to account for the hope that is within
you, yet do it with gentleness and reverence.
—*1 Peter 3:15b–16a*

"You're a false prophet, ma'am, leading your flock to hell!"

At least the protester had manners as he spewed his vitriol at me. It was a beautiful spring day, and we had just wrapped up the groundbreaking ceremony for our new church building in Columbia, South Carolina, where I serve as associate pastor. The older, bearded protester had been accompanied by a younger man who I would have mistaken for a crunchy granola peace protester were it not for his sign proclaiming God's hatred for "sodomites." They had made such a ruckus during our groundbreaking ceremony that I stepped away long enough to call the police—who never showed up.

His verbal attack came as I walked back to my car after the service. I found him and his companion between me and my car after I had hugged the last members of our congregation and sent them on their way. As I approached the pair, I mulled over what to do.

Should I say something? Should I simply nod as I passed? Should I try to engage them in conversation?

I opted for a simple "God bless you, gentlemen. Have a great evening."

It was enough to set him off. The older man began yelling, and I'm pretty sure not one word, except for *ma'am*, was polite. Yet beyond his accusing me of being a false prophet, I honestly don't remember any more of what he said. I was too busy being amazed at how unfazed I was by his words. They zinged past me like bullets. I could hear them whizzing by, none of them ever quite finding their mark. The ones that did seem to make contact made no impression; the sharply pointed words bounced off me like bullets bounced off Superman.

If his attack had come even just a few months earlier, I would have turned on my heel and been nose to nose with him in a heartbeat—giving as good as I got, arguing my point with fervor, and using everything in me to refute his angry words. But in that moment, as his anger blasted out at me, I realized I had reached the goal I had been striving for over the past few years. I had developed a bulletproof faith.

Finally, I had a faith that could take any abuse heaped upon it and still remain strong, a faith that did not need to argue for its survival. This bulletproof faith didn't flinch when others disagreed or condemned it. This faith was grounded in my experience and knowledge of God, not anyone else's opinion about God. I felt like I had finally found the holy grail of spirituality—a faith that could withstand the bullets of condemnation and criticism.

Instead of arguing with the protester, I smiled as I walked to my car where my partner waited with open arms and a warm kiss. We walked arm in arm to the car, the harsh words growing fainter in the distance.

Victories and Defeats

This was just one of the many victories I've celebrated over the years as I have solidified my bulletproof faith. Along with the victories, however, come setbacks, and they should certainly be expected. Attacks on our faith from strangers are just that—the opinion of strangers, which in the long run don't matter very much. Attacks from other quarters, like our church or our family, however, may put a chink in our armor, piercing a still unguarded place in our faith of which we weren't fully aware. Even today

I struggle to heal those weak parts of my faith, especially when attacks come from those closest to me (like family). So I want you to know that as you embark on your own journey to make your faith bulletproof, don't expect overnight results and don't expect that you'll survive every attack intact. The good news is that when a bullet finds an unprotected spot and pierces your heart, you can learn from the experience, heal the vulnerable spot, and become even stronger in your faith. This book is intended to help you identify the areas where the slings and arrows of the world can still penetrate and to give you the tools you need to shield those weak places so that future attacks bounce right off.

A lot of people challenge my faith because I am a lesbian. They tell me I am a false Christian and am inevitably bound for hell because *they* object, for whatever reason, to one portion of my life—my sexual orientation. Those challenges led me to do many things, including founding *Whosoever*, the first online magazine for gay, lesbian, bisexual, and transgender Christians. Those challenges also led me to the Candler School of Theology at Emory University in Atlanta, Georgia, where I received a master of theological studies degree, which led eventually to ordained ministry. It also led me to develop a workshop on spiritual self-defense that I presented at many conferences attended by GLBT Christians. Those challenges planted the seed for this book after participants kept telling me how much they got out of the workshop.

This book is focused on helping the GLBT community develop a bulletproof faith. But I think anyone who is feeling alienated from the church in this time of growing fundamentalism will find something of value here, and you are invited to join us on this journey.

What this book will not do, however, is go deep into the scriptures used against GLBT people of faith. Many wonderful and insightful books have been written on this subject; I provide a list of them at the end of this book. I highly recommend choosing a few of these books and familiarizing yourself with this material. To develop a bulletproof faith, it is essential that you study this material closely so that when someone attacks you with one of the so-called clobber passages,[1] you'll be in a position to respond—if only in your own mind—with reasons why these passages do *not* condemn GLBT people. I cannot overstress the importance of knowing this material. *Whosoever's* "Bible and Homosexuality" section is the most visited part of our site. I have even received letters from people who hang their entire decision on whether or not to accept their sexual orientation as God's gift on the interpretation of these passages. This is important knowledge to acquire as we journey toward a bulletproof faith.

Because it is imperative to a bulletproof faith to make peace with the Bible, I will be addressing the history and context of the Bible itself. Examining the Bible in its proper historical and critical perspective reveals that we have nothing to fear from it. Instead, we find in its pages much joy and affirmation as GLBT people of faith. Reclaiming the Bible, making it our friend, an ally that strengthens instead of weakens our authentic self, is essential to bulletproofing our faith.

This book will provide you with specific tools you can use on your bulletproofing quest, but it doesn't lay out all the answers to attacks or arguments. Why? Because the answers you seek when your faith is challenged are to be found deep inside of you. In a sense, you already know the answers to these attacks and arguments.

The goal of this book, then, is to help you uncover the hidden knowledge buried within you—the internal security of knowing that makes your faith bulletproof when under attack.

The heart of spiritual self-defense is to learn how to shift focus from *defense* to *self*. I define *defense* as the outward actions we take when arguments or attacks come—the words we use, the way we say them, and the forcefulness of our arguments. I define *self* as that true place where God resides in all of us, or as Steven Pressfield calls it in *The Legend of Bagger Vance*, our "authentic swing."[2]

Pressfield's book, and the subsequent movie of the same name, tells the story of a troubled golfer from Savannah,

Georgia, who is invited to take part in an exhibition game in 1931 that features two more accomplished golfers. Rannulph Junah is accompanied by his mysterious caddie, Bagger Vance. The main plot revolves around the golf match, but the book is not really about golf. Instead, it is about uncovering and delving into the authentic self that lives deep within. Throughout the book, Vance leads a hesitant Junah on the path of self-discovery by tutoring him not so much on the finer points of golf as on the finer points of a life lived in authenticity. "Each of us possesses, inside ourselves, one true Authentic Swing that is ours alone," Vance tells Junah.[3] But it must be coaxed from the unconscious into self-awareness and finally to enlightenment. This is the path we are called to take if we are to develop a bulletproof faith.

You've Got Hate Mail!

Following is an example of the type of hate messages that have landed in my e-mail inbox over the years. I have combined some typical phrases that crop up most often in hate mail. These are clichés we've heard over and over again, including "love the sinner, hate the sin," "you weren't born that way," "stop justifying your lifestyle with the Bible," and the contention that AIDS is a punishment from God for being gay. Read this composite hate message, and make note of your gut reactions. Then I'd like you to write a response to this e-mail. We'll revisit it at the end of the book:

> As a Christian, God tells me not to judge others. I love the sinner and hate the sin, but you're wrong to believe that God made you gay. These are lies from the enemy, straight from the pit of hell. You are SO going straight to Hell, you ignorant, misguided, perverted misfit! Not only for choosing this abomination of a lifestyle, but for trying

> to promote it through the very book it flies
> in the face of. You make me and God want to
> vomit! AIDS is a cure!

When I founded *Whosoever* in 1996, I was immediately beset by hate mail—the kind I've just presented and much worse. Threats of death—wishes for my swift descent into hell—arrived in my mailbox daily. It was unnerving, to say the least.

Every single time I'd open up a piece of mail, my heart would pound. I would get lightheaded. I would get angry as I read the words of condemnation that spilled from the keyboards of men and women who professed to be followers of Christ. More often than not, I responded with the same level of vitriol. I defended myself by lashing back—by calling them names, by questioning the sincerity of their faith, by lowering myself to their level. I was attacked, and I fought back. I saw absolutely nothing wrong with that behavior.

Then I read a very interesting passage in my Bible, the one that opened this chapter: "Always be prepared to make a defense to any one who calls you to account for the hope that is within you, yet do it with gentleness and reverence" (1 Peter 3:15b–16a).

Gentleness and reverence? You've got to be kidding! Not a single attacker has shown *me* any gentleness or reverence. It's been a steady stream of hatred, vitriol, cruelty, threats, and just plain rudeness! Why should I reward insolence with "gentleness and reverence"?

It took a long time for me to come to understand why we should indeed follow Peter's sage advice. Consistently responding to attacks, no matter how devastating, with gentleness and reverence is the only way to approach spiritual self-defense.

Don't Commit Spiritual Suicide

When I first wrote on the idea of spiritual self-defense in 1998 in an issue of *Whosoever*, I compared my approach to that of the martial art of aikido. In aikido, there are no offensive moves—you

cannot attack someone with aikido; you can only react to some-one attacking you. That does not mean that aikido is not a deadly martial art. You can indeed kill an attacker who contin-ues to come at you.

While I do not recommend that you challenge anyone to a "battle to the death," I do want to impress on you just how seriously we must take the art of spiritual self-defense. We must recognize that there are attackers out there who wish to see us dead—and if not physically, at least spiritually. We must learn to defend ourselves no matter what—our spiritual, physical, and mental health depends on it.

If we fail at spiritual self-defense, however, it will not be because the other person "beat" us or "won" the argument. It will be simply because we surrendered and tossed up our hands in defeat. The Danish theologian Søren Kierkegaard wrote in *Works of Love* that there is no such thing as a spiritual murder. "Certainly no violent assaulter can murder an immortal spirit," he writes. "Spiritually, suicide is the only possible death."[4]

The bullets of others can wound us deeply, but we are the only ones who can put the final, fatal bullet into the heart of our faith. We see it in the GLBT community all the time. We see it in "ex-gay" movements that tell us we can change and then blame our lack of faith when the change ultimately fails. We see it in mainstream churches where we're told it's OK for us to sit in the pew but we're not good enough to be ordained or to hold leadership positions because surely God would not call someone like us. We are led into spiritual suicide. We give up, reason-ing, "Well, if the church doesn't want me, then I don't want the church."

I followed this path myself when I was sixteen. If God hated me because I was a lesbian, fine, I could hate God just as easily. I killed my own spirit. I pushed it out, alienated it, and turned my back on God. The good news is that our spirit is immortal—and able to be resurrected. It is my desire that your faith finds resurrection in these pages and tools to revitalize that faith.

Training Not to Fight

One of the things that always irritated me about learning aikido is that all the instructors focused on the outside actions one takes in defense and not the inside actions one must take for oneself. Aikido, like any martial art, can be very effective if you know only the outward motions. But it becomes a way of life, a more effective mode of being, when you focus just as much attention—or more—on the inside, or what is called *chi*.

Without *chi*, one cannot attain a true balance between the inner world and the outer world. In the movie *The Karate Kid*, this balance is highlighted in the differences between how Mr. Miyagi trains Daniel and how the more militant karate instructor trains his kids. Miyagi teaches Daniel such seemingly meaningless chores as waxing his cars and painting his fence. Daniel is learning the right moves, but he's also building his skill from the inside, finding his center, his *chi*.

In one scene, Daniel, upset at the outward power and bravado of the other karate kids, questions Miyagi's methods. Like all young people, he's certain that the aged Miyagi has never faced the kinds of problems he's facing, so he asks Miyagi if he fought when he was young. Miyagi assures him that he fought a lot when he was younger and was always scared because he hated fighting. That puzzles Daniel. He wonders how a master of a martial art could hate fighting. For Miyagi, however, training in karate is not about training to fight. Instead, as Daniel finally figures out, you train so you won't have to fight.

We do not train in spiritual self-defense so that we can get in the ring and show off our skill. Instead, we train, we learn, we find that balance within ourselves for one reason only: so that we don't have to fight.

When I began seminary in 1998, I went with one purpose: to learn how to fight. I wanted to learn everything I could about the history of Christianity, about the Bible and theology, so that I could respond to those who told me I could not be both a lesbian and a Christian. I wanted answers. I wanted to have the skill to fight—to show off what I had learned and most of all to win each and every battle.

At the end of my seminary career, I was required to write a paper integrating my experiences in school. My dean told me it would be good to write about what brought me to seminary. What questions did I have when I arrived, and what answers did I have at the end of my seminary career?

"I came here to learn how to answer those who told me I couldn't be both gay and Christian," I said.

"Well, what's your answer?" he asked.

Like Daniel, I thought for a minute before saying, "I don't have to answer them."

I had arrived at an amazing place. I did all this training, spoiling for a fight. Yet in the end, I realized that my training was done so that I would never have to fight. My training taught me that it is not the outside, where the arguments take place, that should be my focus, but rather inside, where the arguments are settled once and for all. What my training taught me is that I had put the wrong emphasis on self-defense. Instead of *defense*, I needed to focus on *self*. Only then could my faith become bulletproof.

At the heart of a bulletproof faith (regardless of one's gender, one's sexual identity, or any socially constructed difference humans invent) is a divine assurance that we are worthy of God's love, care, and blessing. We need not do anything special to deserve God's grace. We need to trust that God believes we are special for no other reason than because we are here. Our very existence proves our worthiness. God has created all things, even things that certain other of his creatures may shun or marginalize.

Any messages telling us we are unworthy or unloved are, simply put, lies.

"We easily hear an inner voice calling us evil, bad, rotten, worthless, useless, doomed to sickness and death," wrote Henri

Nouwen in *Life of the Beloved*. "Isn't it easier for us to believe that we are cursed than that we are blessed? Still I say to you, as the Beloved [Child] of God, you are blessed. Good words are being spoken about you—words that tell the truth. The curses—noisy, boisterous, loud-mouthed as they may be—do not tell the truth. They are lies; lies easy to believe, but lies nevertheless."[5]

It is my hope that by the end of this book, you will have not only the tools you need to develop your own bulletproof faith but also the unshakable knowledge that you are a beloved, blessed child of God, which is of course what you are.

Spiritual Survival Tips

1. Developing a bulletproof faith is a process, long and non-linear. It may involve taking one step forward and two steps back. There will always be chinks in your armor that will need repair. Stay vigilant.

2. Trust the inner voice that guides you. If you do, you'll discover you know how to defend your faith already. Know that your inner voice is God revealed in your authentic self. Trust that voice above all others.

3. Respond to any and all attacks with gentleness and reverence. Resist the temptation to respond with the same viciousness with which you are attacked. Show love to everyone you meet.

4. Resist the temptation to let the opinion of others lead you to spiritual suicide. No attack, no matter how violent or severe, can kill your faith. Only you have the power to kill your faith.

5. Do not seek a bulletproof faith so that you can flaunt your strength or to try to defeat others in battle. Instead, seek to become bulletproof so that you no longer feel the need to fight.

2

LOSING OUR RELIGION

God created us because God thought we might
enjoy it.

—*Hazel Glover, Episcopal priest and good friend*

I learned a long time ago to give up anything that makes you
cry. Misery is God's way of telling you that this isn't the path
you should follow.

When I was in my twenties, I worked at telemarketing jobs
in between radio gigs to make ends meet. I was good, but I hated
it. The rejection was just too much, and my skin was too thin. I
came home crying almost every day. I had to give it up.

In my thirties, I was working at CNN—a dream job by journalism standards—but again, I reached a point where I simply
couldn't do it anymore. I came home most nights crying. The
business I had loved for two decades had so changed that I felt I
was no longer a journalist but what Steven Pressfield in his book
The War of Art calls a hack: "When the hack sits down to work,
he doesn't ask himself what's in his own heart. He asks what the
market is looking for. . . . You've sold out your Muse, and your
Muse is you, the best part of yourself, where your finest and only
true work comes from."[1]

I had sold out my Muse at CNN, writing what my bosses told
me the market demanded—infotainment that passed as news.
It ate away at my soul and left me feeling hollow and violated
by the end of the day. I had to leave a job that most journalists
would kill for because it was literally killing *me*.

In my forties, while working in academic public relations, I
again came home crying, feeling defeated by a JAVA programming
class that I had subjected myself to in the name of improving my

computer skills and perhaps making yet another career change. As my past experiences have shown me, if something makes me miserable, it must stop. So I quit school. However, several days after this decision, my boss came to me and told me she'd like to spend a little money sending me to some computer classes to expand the work I could do for the organization. When I stopped doing things that made me cry, the resources I had searched for found their way to me by another path. Suddenly, I realized I was following the right road—one I would enjoy.

"God created us because God thought we might enjoy it." Those are wise words from my Episcopalian friend—words we should always remember. If we're not enjoying our lives, we must root out the source of our misery and get rid of it. When we stop forcing ourselves to do things that make us miserable—even if the world says what we're doing is a good thing—it's like ceasing to pound our hand with a hammer. It feels so good to stop. This is not an "if it feels good, do it" philosophy but instead a way of learning to pay attention to our own internal warning signs that we're off track.

There's nothing wrong with being a telemarketer, a journalist, or a computer programmer if you love the work and feel called to do it, but if it makes you cry at night, give it up. Anything that makes you miserable is not part of your true calling—your authentic self.

The best day of my life, however, was when I gave up religion that made me cry. This is when I began the hard work of finding my authentic self—differentiating it from the self that had been given to me by my family and my Southern Baptist religion. It took years to get to that day, years of self-loathing, years of crying out to God to be changed into something I was not created to be, years of listening to teachers and preachers tell me that God would hate me if I went looking for my authentic self. I spent years listening to a religion that told me the authentic self I sensed underneath the dogma and doctrine was an abomination. I spent years believing that my authentic self was something hated by God—something that needed to be changed. When I finally stopped listening to and believing the voices outside of me and instead turned inward and listened to the voice of God within myself, I learned the truth—and I stopped crying. I discovered that my true self was the one that God had given me, no matter what religious leaders had to say.

Easier Said Than Done

It sounds good to say, "I gave up all the stuff that made me cry and now I'm happier," but it's mighty hard to do. I get letters from many miserable GLBT people because they cannot give up religious beliefs that make them cry. They're convinced that being miserable is a normal state because that's what their religion has taught them. Christian theologians teach us that we must "sacrifice" to please God, that we must "deny ourselves" (Mark 8:34) to be a follower of Christ.

I've spent a lot of time on Internet message boards arguing with fundamentalist Christians about these subjects. One man I talked with over the years was incredibly morose. He believed that denying oneself, taking up the cross, and following God meant that God wanted us to live in misery. He could not even enjoy a joke because to him, it was against God to laugh or enjoy life. To him, sacrifice and denying oneself meant that one must be serious, humorless, and absolutely joyless to follow God. His story reminded me of Martin Luther, who regarded himself as "a stinking bag of worms" before God.[2]

What a contrast from the demands Jesus himself made of his followers. Jesus told his disciples that he came so that we might have life, and have it in abundance! Living as "worms" does not glorify God, and it does not reflect the abundance Jesus said he came to give us. Jesus makes it clear in Matthew 9:13 that what is demanded of us is not sacrifice but mercy. A religion bent on making us miserable and making us cry is devoid of mercy (or "steadfast love," as some translations read) and does not reflect Jesus' message.

As for Jesus' command to deny ourselves if we are to be his followers, I can't believe for a second that Jesus means that we must deny our sexual orientation. Obviously, this is not a call for our heterosexual counterparts to deny *their* sexual orientation. Instead, what Jesus demands is for us to leave behind our human penchant for self-absorption. We have to stop believing, "It's all about me." Instead, we should learn how to love God with all our heart, mind, and soul and to love our neighbor (which means everyone, by the way) as much as we love ourselves (Matthew 22:37–40).

We cannot love our neighbor if we are absorbed in our own lives. We cannot follow Christ if we are constantly thinking, "What's in it for me?" Instead of denying ourselves the abundance of life, Jesus is telling us to give up our selfishness so that we can enjoy life to the fullest. Saint Francis of Assisi nailed this paradox perfectly: "It's in giving that we receive." When we step outside of ourselves, give up our selfish desires for more stuff, and instead focus on how we can be of service to others, we are taking the first steps to "denying ourselves" so that we may properly follow Christ.

But as GLBT people, we understand what it feels like to be "stinking bags of worms." We have been made to feel we are unworthy of God's love. That's the message that's blasted at us from the pulpit, from our families, and often from complete strangers. We're constantly told that our hearts are bad, that our love is "disordered," and that we must change to be loved by God. We take these judgments to heart, assuming they must be true. We abandon God and religion altogether because, really, who would want to feel that way about themselves? We'd rather walk away from such toxic ideas than embrace a system that perpetuates them. Even when we walk away, however, the messages stay with us. This can cause internalized homophobia—a sense of shame and loathing for our authentic self. These internalized messages of shame are simmering under the surface all the time. We believe our heart is bad, stained black as coal. We don't understand that beneath that black veneer lurks a diamond—a heart that is good because it is created and loved by God.

Diamonds form from lumps of coal as the result of heat and pressure. As we uncover the diamond below the surface—our authentic self—we must undergo trials. We must feel the heat and the pressure of life. We will be scorned, mocked, rejected, attacked, and perhaps physically assaulted for being who we are. Instead of letting those hardships overwhelm us, we must allow God to use this raw material to shape us into the unique self that shines with God's glory.

John Eldredge, in *Waking the Dead*, reminds us, "God endowed you with a glory when he created you, a glory so deep and mythic that all creation pales in comparison. A glory unique to you, just as your fingerprints are unique to you, just as the way you laugh is unique to you. Somewhere down deep inside we've been looking for that glory ever since."[3]

Eldredge talks about our unique "glory"—or our authentic self. This is what we constantly seek as human beings, regardless of sexual orientation or gender identity. We aren't born bad, with an original stain on our souls. God tells us we are good—created in God's image and proclaimed a good creation. Our glory—or authentic self—is a reflection of God. But we don't remember that. We get caught up in the religious image of a "wretch," and we forget that God said we were good.

Brilliance and Fire

When we buy into the belief that we are "stinking bags of worms" before God, we make what Eldredge calls "agreements" with the enemy of our heart. Eldredge believes in a personified "devil" that is our enemy. I believe our worst enemy is ourselves—our very human nature, our self-absorption, the part of us that is ready to believe the worst and doubt the best about ourselves.

Whichever image you hold of the "enemy," the reality of such an enemy is undeniable. There always seems to be something out there ready to sabotage our happiness, ready to cut us down when we begin to believe that our heart is good and that God loves us unconditionally. Whether it's a literal devil or self-sabotage is not important. What is important is learning to overcome the negative tapes constantly playing in our heads. We must change them into positive messages that edify us instead of cripple us.

I know that enemy well. I have a short temper in traffic. Once, after cursing out a fellow driver, I made agreements all the way home with the enemy that is my selfish ego. "You're an idiot," the voice said. "How can you be a good person, a pastor even, and say such horrible things to people? Your heart is bad, because out of the heart comes your words, and what words were the first to pop into your head? Filthy words—not words of blessing or grace or peace or hope or joy. No, you cursed instead of blessed. You wanted to say more, really tell him off; you simply didn't have time to show how truly horrible you are."

On and on it went. I felt terrible. The enemy was attacking me—lowering my self-esteem, making me hate and doubt myself. How could I be a pastor—someone who told others how they ought to live—and yet words of peace were not the first ones out of my own mouth? I had to agree. I was a horrible person. Someone who ought not be a pastor. Perhaps I should quit.

See where this line of thinking leads? Of course the enemy wants me to quit. Of course the enemy wants me to feel unworthy to serve God. If I feel that way, the enemy wins. I hang it up, and that's one less person talking about God's love for everyone. That's one less person talking about God's desire for everyone to understand that his or her heart is good.

I had to shake myself and realize that this voice did not come from God. The voice in my head was the voice of self-defeat, self-doubt, self-loathing, self-absorption. That voice is in all of us, calling us to give up on God, calling us to give up on loving ourselves, much less loving our neighbor. That voice tells us our heart is bad, and more often than not, we agree.

Eldredge warns against making these agreements. The enemy will suggest all sorts of things, telling us that God doesn't care about us, that we're not worthy of God's love, that we can't trust God. The enemy, Eldredge says, "is trying to kill your heart, destroy the glory in your life. It will feel hard—really hard, almost impossible—but whatever you do, make no agreements. You have to start there."[4]

Never again would we make any agreement that we are not worthy of God's love if we understood the process God uses to uncover the shimmering diamond of God's glory within each of us. We are diamonds in the rough, but diamonds have two properties that a master cutter can bring forth. First, a diamond has brilliance. It is "the fraction of light that falls on [it] that the diamond returns to the eyes of an observer—the more light returned, the higher the brilliance."[5] Our brilliance is how much of God's love we shine into the world. The brighter our brilliance, the more of Christ's light people see shining from our lives. You've met people that seem to shine with love and joy. Those are the brilliant diamonds that God, the master cutter, has created.

Second, a diamond has fire. This is the diamond's "ability to split white light into rainbow colors—the greater the separation of between colors, the greater the fire."[6] If any community has fire, it's the GLBT community. Our ability to project rainbow colors in the world is legendary. We are on fire when are working in the world not just for the full inclusion of GLBT people in church and society but for the inclusion of everyone—even those who may work against us. Martin Luther King Jr. had that kind of fire as he sought to turn even the worst racist into his friend. This is the kind of fire that God can bring forth from us as we undergo the heat and pressure of the trials that come to us.

The job of the master cutter is to enhance both the fire and the brilliance of a diamond. This is how God works in our lives, cutting away anything that hampers us from expressing our authentic selves in the world. God cuts away the prejudices, the selfishness, the hostility, the jealousy, the pettiness, the grudges, the fears, the hurts, the despair, the joylessness, and the hopelessness and brings forth the original glory that we all possess. God, the master cutter, reveals our love, our generosity, our joy, our hope, our courage, and our compassion. God equips us to help heal the world by shining forth with brilliance and fire.

We are all diamonds, every single one of us. We just don't know it. Or we do know it but have forgotten it. We believe the lies that say we're just old black pieces of coal. We scorn ourselves endlessly, something Louis Evely warns against in *That Man Is You:*

> God alone knows what He expects from us, what response He's looking for and how many people's destinies depend on ours. When we scorn ourselves, we scorn all those plans of His, all the dreams He was going to realize through us, all the joy He anticipated from us. Each of us is a piece of property that belongs to God but is entrusted to us. We hardly ever know of what use it is, and as a rule, He's careful not to tell us. Quite naturally we wonder what it can possibly be for and who or what can ever really benefit from our life. Faith makes us believe that God deems it useful, necessary for His projects and indispensable to His joy.[7]

After my traffic altercation, I sure didn't feel my brilliance or my fire. I wasn't sure what benefit anyone or anything could get from my life, and God wasn't telling. In that moment, I could rely on nothing but my faith and the assurance, deep in my soul, that God loved me—that I belonged to God—even if I was ill-tempered. I had to remember that God is still at work in me, cutting away all the anger so that my brilliance and fire can shine through.

This is our role as diamonds, to remind not just ourselves but everyone we encounter of the fire and brilliance within us all. When I founded *Whosoever*, I told myself that if just one person discovered that diamond lurking within, the magazine would have done its job. By that measure, *Whosoever* has been success-ful beyond my wildest dreams. I get so many e-mails from people telling me how much *Whosoever* has meant to them. More than one reader has told me that they were about to commit sui-cide, but something they read in the magazine gave them hope. Others have told me that they had walked away from God but discovered they could finally be gay, lesbian, bisexual, or trans-gender and still have God in their lives simply because of the resources the magazine provides. Still others realized that God created them as they are and loves them that way. All of them have discovered that they are diamonds and must allow their brilliance and fire to light the path for others.

It's not necessary to found an Internet magazine or other public ministry to reach people in this way. We can start right now with the people in our lives. Encourage a family mem-ber who is feeling down. Look for opportunities to lift up anyone who may be in despair or feeling alone or depressed. Take every chance to reach out to others. We must be about the business of reminding all who cross our path that they are God's precious diamonds and are meant to shine their brilliance and fire into the world.

Watch Your Language

To reveal our glory, we must break agreements that tell us we are worthless and will always remain that way. To do that, we've got to work on how we think and how we talk. Right speech is important if we're going to reveal our glory not just to ourselves but to everyone.

Our first practice in right speech should be in prayer—right speech to God. "The most efficacious deed we can perform is prayer," Evely says, "for it's in the active passivity of prayer that everything's decided and everything takes shape."[8]

Prayer also keeps us from being too puffed up about ourselves, thinking that what we accomplish is entirely the result of our own effort. Prayer keeps us from falling into the "my stuff don't stink" trap. Prayer keeps us humble and reminds us who is really in charge of our lives and the world. Any good we accomplish is possible because God is working through us. God is using our talents, our skills, our willingness, and our capacity to serve to accomplish what God intends in the world.

The Fourth Mindfulness Training observed by Buddhists reads, "Aware of the suffering caused by unmindful speech and the inability to listen to others, I am committed to cultivating loving speech and deep listening in order to bring joy and happiness to others and relieve others of their suffering. I will refrain from uttering words that cause division or discord."[9] This is very close to Jesus' warning in Matthew 12:34–37 that our words will either acquit us or condemn us. Right speech is imperative. When we face difficult people, we must respond to them with gentleness and reverence. In this way, we learn to watch our language and avoid being condemned by our own words.

Whenever we encounter people who tell us we cannot be both GLBT and Christian, we need to remember that whatever we say to them should be edifying and not combative. For example, if someone says, "I love the sinner, but I just hate the sin," one approach to using right speech could be to respond, "I agree. We should love everyone because God has created us all and has created us good. I also agree that sin is something we should all seek to avoid. We may disagree on what constitutes a sin, but we agree that God loves us no matter how much we may fall short of God's goals for us."

Such a response defuses a potentially harmful situation. Instead of immediately becoming defensive, we are seeking to find common ground with our opponent. Often the speaker doesn't even realize that what he or she is saying is offensive.

The person may not be spoiling for a fight but instead have not been educated in how to speak to or about GLBT people. If we can find ways to affirm our opponents and genuinely agree with some of what they are saying, they may soften their stance or come to realize that though we may disagree on some things, there is far more common ground between us than they may have realized.

We must remember as well that sometimes right speech means no speech at all. If a person continues to attack or wants to provoke a pointless argument, our best response may be silence. In such instances, we can thank them for their opinion and leave the conversation. There is no reason to continue to engage in conversation with someone who insists on abusing us or calling names.

Walking the Walk

Watching our language is only half the battle to revealing our glory—our authentic self. We must also learn the best way to walk. I'm not talking about how you literally walk but about how you walk in life. Does your walk show others your glory? Does your walk reveal the light of God to others, or does your walk show that you still believe yourself to be an unrefined piece of coal, stained by false ideas of a horrible, sinful nature?

Years ago, while working at a low-paying radio job, I took a side job in retail. The supervisor who hired me was a friend from church—I'll call him Rick. He warned me that he had not told anyone at work that he was gay and would appreciate my discretion around other employees. I respected his wishes but soon found out that his sexual orientation was the worst-kept secret around the store. Everyone knew that Rick was gay and routinely made fun of him and laughed at his attempts to cover up the truth about himself. As a result, no one on his staff trusted him. They felt that if he would lie to them about something so intrinsic to his very being, what else would he feel free to be dishonest about?

I told Rick what the employees said about him behind his back, but he was not swayed. His goal was to attain a higher-powered job within the corporation, and he felt that hiding this part of his authentic self was the best way to achieve that goal.

I lost a lot of respect for Rick in that experience, but what grieved me more is the fact that Rick is like so many GLBT people who believe they cannot present their authentic selves to the world. In many ways, it's not Rick's fault. He's simply bought into society's lie that GLBT people are somehow deeply flawed and that to gain acceptance or have a successful career, they must hide their sexual orientation or gender identity. Rick's priority was a cushy corporate job, and he was willing to walk a path of denial to get there. He's not alone; many GLBT people follow that path, selling out their authentic selves for career advancement or to secure their place within the church or their families. Hiding, using elusive pronouns, and telling outright lies becomes a way of life.

I know that way of life well. I was open about my sexual orientation while I worked for Rick, but that wasn't always the case. Early in my radio career, I, too, was deep inside the closet. I hid, used elusive pronouns like *we* and *us* and outright lied about my life. The radio station where I worked was in a conservative town in northeastern Georgia. I was on the air, covering news stories and hosting a talk show. I believed that if I had been honest about my sexual orientation, I would have lost my job.

For that reason and others, I was miserable in that job and looked to the Atlanta market to save me. I was honest about my sexual orientation in interviews, and no one blinked an eye. When I finally landed a job, I was pleasantly surprised on my first night on the job to meet two other lesbians in the newsroom. From that day forward, I stopped hiding and only took jobs where my sexual orientation was not an issue. I learned to walk with integrity—bringing my authentic self into my career. I found I was always respected, not just for my talent but also for the integrity of my walk.

In later years, however, I discovered that even though I believed I had done a great job at concealing my sexual orientation, a former coworker told me my lesbianism was common knowledge at my old station. Everyone knew—and no one cared. I could have been honest about my sexual orientation there, but I was too afraid to be who God made me to be. I lost the respect of many of my coworkers; even more important, I lost respect for myself. Like Rick, I was walking a false path. I felt ashamed of my sexual orientation because society teaches that there is something intrinsically wrong with anyone who is attracted to people of their same gender. I believed that view and internalized it, feeling ashamed of my authentic self. I, like Rick, felt I had to hide part of my true self if I wanted to get ahead in my career.

Now I seek to walk with integrity in every area of my life. This is how I reveal my glory, my authentic self, to the world. When we walk in integrity, bringing the full power of our authentic self into every area of our lives, our original glory cannot help but shine through. Our authentic self can provide light in the darkness of people's lives, joy where there is misery, hope where there is doubt, love where there is hatred, and peace where there is turmoil. If we'll search and find the best way to walk, we'll find that simply living our lives is how we best reveal the glory God has freely given us.

The Glory of Community

Working on revealing our glory can be a very private endeavor in many ways because we are working to embrace the goodness of our own heart. However, our glory—that authentic self—will never fully be revealed until we are part of a community of seekers who also are striving to uncover their innate glory. We must be in community to grow in love, practice right speech, and walk in love and light.

I've tried living outside of this type of community before. There was a time when I could not feel at home in a church or any group gathering. I wanted to live a hermit's life. I found it easy, given all of our modern conveniences. While living in Atlanta, I discovered a wonderful (but now sadly defunct) invention called Webvan, an online grocery delivery service. You'd do your shopping online, and a delivery person would bring in the bags of groceries, run your debit card, and leave with a hearty thank you. I only had to leave the house for work. If my job had allowed telecommuting (and Webvan had been allowed by law to deliver beer), I would never have left the house.

My soul atrophied during this time. I was lonely but determined to stick it out. I had been hurt by the church too many times. I had witnessed too many power struggles, too much infighting, too much bickering to trust my heart to that again. I shut myself away, determined to grow spiritually on my own. It didn't work. I became bitter, cynical, more convinced than ever that I was an worthless piece of coal. I was unable to even fathom becoming a diamond.

Being in community can be messy and hard. There are always feelings being hurt or intentions being misinterpreted or someone feeling left out. We must remember, though, that it takes a lot of muck, mud, heat, and pressure to form a diamond. Community is the best resource we have for uncovering our authentic self, and it is worth fighting for because we are stronger together than we are apart.

Take *Buffy the Vampire Slayer*, for example. In the television series, Buffy is the "Chosen One" of prophecy—the one woman in the world endowed with the powers needed to fight and defeat vampires. In one episode, Buffy and her friends battled a Frankenstein-like monster created out of demon parts. He was virtually invincible. The only way to kill him was to destroy his battery pack, lodged deep in his chest. The monster, ironically named Adam, had been created as part of a secret Army project. His strength was greater than Buffy's by herself. Buffy, however, was determined to face the monster alone, rejecting any assistance from her friends. In one scene, Buffy and her friends quarrel, exchanging angry words, accusations, and recriminations.

Buffy storms out of the room telling them she understands why the prophecy foretold of a chosen "one" and didn't mention any friends.

Later on, Willow, the witch of the group, finds a spell to defeat Adam. There is only one catch: they must all be involved. While Willow, Giles, and Xander work together to create the spell invoking the power of the first vampire slayer, Buffy goes to battle against Adam. When the spell takes over, Buffy is imbued with great power—an original glory bestowed on the first slayer and transferred to her through the efforts of her friends. She is able to defeat Adam, telling him that she is filled with a power greater than his. The power did not come to her on her own but was discovered in the power of community. With the help of the people who knew her most intimately, she was able to fully reveal her glory and defeat the enemy.

And so it is with us. We must live in community. That community should know us well and understand that our hearts are good. Being in community is always challenging and fraught with conflict. If we believe that our own heart is good and that the hearts of those in our community are good, we will understand that community always brings out our best.

Just as Jesus sent his disciples to heal in his name and spread the word about God's unconditional love, so God sends us into the world to be God's hands, feet, eyes, and arms. Our hearts are good, and we must tell others that theirs are good as well. We can do that with our words, certainly, but our actions speak louder. This is where we get to display our fire—shining our rainbow colors into the world. We must always look for ways to serve others—whether it's volunteering at a community service, helping someone mow the lawn, or simply letting someone ahead of us in line. We must outdo one another in service and love.

We are called to move out of ourselves and our tendency to hide out and make ourselves available to serve everyone in God's creation. If we are to be great, if we are to reveal our glory, we must come forth, live in community, and seek to be God's instruments of service in the world. Until we do that, we are no better than pieces of coal. We cannot be diamonds unless we are willing to be out in the world, shimmering with the brilliance and fire of God's glory reflecting from our souls.

Start by Saying No

Begin your journey now by breaking all the agreements you've made with the voice in your head telling you God can't possibly love a stinking bag of worms like you. Say no the next time that voice tells you that God hates you because you're gay or lesbian or bisexual or transgender. Say no the next time that voice tells you that you're not good enough to be one of God's children. Say no the next time that voice in your head tells you that no community will have you. Say no the next time that voice in your head tells you that you have nothing to give to anyone else. Say no the next time that voice tells you that your heart is bad and you are stained with original sin. Don't make these agreements.

Instead, cultivate the voice that tells you that you are good, you are loved, and you are created just the way God intended you to be—good and full of glory. There will be times, like my blow-up in traffic, where you'll slip and begin to hear that voice telling you you're no good. Don't believe it. Understand the voice for what it is—the enemy trying to undermine you, trying to get you to abandon the fact that you are imbued with God's wonderful glory. Even if you fail on occasion, don't believe the lie that your heart is full of evil. It's not; your heart is good.

Spiritual Survival Tips

1. Give up all religious beliefs that make you cry or diminish your self-esteem. If a belief does not edify and uplift you, it is not a good belief. Jesus came to give us abundant life, a life to enjoy to the fullest.

2. Give up self-absorption. Find new ways to step outside of yourself and serve God and neighbor.

3. Break any agreement that tells you that you are not worthy of God's love. Replace negative self-talk with positive self-talk, assuring yourself of God's steadfast love for you, no matter what.

4. Use right speech in prayer and in daily life. Remember, our words can either condemn or acquit.

5. Learn to walk with integrity so that your glory, your authentic self, can shine through to the world.

6. Find a strong, accepting community dedicated to helping you discover your authentic self. Whether it's a brick-and-mortar community in your neighborhood or a virtual community online, these groups are vital to helping us become the diamonds God created us to be.

7. Let no one tell you that God condemns or abhors you. Always remember that your heart is good. God has created you for abundance and joy.

SPIRITUAL SURVIVAL EXERCISE: RECLAIMING YOUR AUTHENTIC SELF

You have, inside of you, something that makes you unique, different from everyone else—an authentic swing. You know it innately. You've probably felt it before but haven't been able to recapture it. The best way I've found to uncover this authentic swing is through a dedicated practice of meditation. Some people resist the idea of meditation because they believe it is either a waste of time just sitting around with your eyes closed or an Eastern practice that isn't proper or necessary for Christians. But the Bible tells us to "be still and know that I am God." Being still is nothing more than the practice of meditation. The meditation we are about to do has its roots in centuries of Christian prayer and tradition.

The benefits of meditation have been reported for centuries, but science has recently proved many of them, including stress reduction and increased focus and attention. Researchers at the University of Wisconsin studied monks in a monastery in India using instruments to measure brain waves while they meditated. They discovered that the abbot of the monastery "had the highest amount of activity in the brain centers associated with positive emotions that had ever been measured by his laboratory," according to Tenzin Gyatso, the fourteenth Dalai Lama.[1]

That doesn't mean you have to go to a monastery or dedicate hours and hours of your life to meditation. A little goes a long way. Researchers at the university taught mindfulness meditation techniques to people who did not practice Buddhism and discovered that even in a short time, their brains changed.

Within eight weeks of starting a meditation practice, researches found that the areas of the brain that generate positive emotions became more active.

Gyatso concluded, "The implications of all this are clear: the world today needs citizens and leaders who can work toward ensuring stability and engage in dialogue with the 'enemy'— no matter what kind of aggression or assault they may have endured."[2]

We can only engage in dialogue with those who oppose us when we are calm and collected within ourselves. A regular practice of meditation can help us remain calm—able to give a gentle and reverent response whenever we are challenged, no matter how severe the attack. Regular meditation keeps us connected with God and connected with that authentic self that is infused with God. This is the fire and brilliance we offer to the world.

Praying the Name of Jesus

The words of the "Jesus Prayer" are taken from a variety of scriptures. The blind man at the side of the road near Jericho who cried out, "Jesus, son of David, have mercy on me" (Luke 18:38) and the ten lepers who said to Jesus, "Master, have pity on us" (Luke 17:13) are two stories incorporated in the prayer.

Another scriptural basis for the prayer is Luke 18:10–14, which tells of a Pharisee and a tax collector who arrived at the temple to pray. The Pharisee, a well-respected man of the day, felt good about his position in society. He was a faithful member of the temple, tithing on all that he earned. He was so happy about his life that he thanked God for not making him like all the others—"extortioners, unjust, adulterers, or even like this tax collector." The tax collector, however, stood far off from the altar and could not even bring himself to look toward heaven. Instead, he beat his breast saying, "God, be merciful to me, a sinner!"

According to Jesus, the tax collector went home justified before God because he did not exalt himself. He did not feel that he was better than anyone. Instead, he understood that before God, we are all the same—standing in the need of forgiveness and humility.

The words of the blind man, the lepers, and this humble tax collector have been repeated over and over again as the "Jesus Prayer." It has been practiced for centuries. The full prayer itself was first found in a sixth-century book called *The Life of Abba Philemon*.[3] Albert Rossi, a clinical psychologist and director of the doctor of ministry program at Saint Vladimir's Orthodox Theological Seminary in Crestwood, New York, described the prayer this way: "The Jesus Prayer is also called the Prayer of the Heart. There is within us a space, a field of the heart, in which we find a Divine Reality, and from which we are called to live. The mind, then, is to descend into that inner sanctuary, by means of the Jesus Prayer or wordless contemplation, and to stay there throughout our active day and evening. We descend with our mind into our heart, and we live there."[4]

That space in our heart where we are called to live is our authentic self or authentic swing. This is where our deepest connection to God occurs. This is where we understand that we can never exalt ourselves. Here we understand that giving thanks to God that we are not like those we dislike are vain, egotistical prayers. Here we understand that God makes no distinction between us and our enemies. Within the inner sanctuary of our authentic self, we finally understand God's unconditional love for all God's creation.

The Jesus Prayer can be a valuable tool to help us uncover that authentic self and enter into that inner sanctuary. The words of the ancient prayer often vary from Luke's words. Instead of simply "God, be merciful to me, a sinner," some use a longer version, praying, "Lord Jesus Christ, Son of God, have mercy on me, a sinner." The reason for making the prayer longer is that it is a breath prayer. As we pray, we synchronize our breath to the prayer, inhaling as we address Jesus, "Lord Jesus Christ, Son of God." As we exhale, we pray, "have mercy on me, a sinner." Many people repeat the sentence silently for fifteen to twenty minutes each day at a specific time they set aside for contemplative prayer. Others simply pray it throughout the day as time permits, such as on their lunch break, during their commute, or while they exercise.

The prayer's structure has two parts: the address and the supplication. In the first part, we address Jesus: "Lord Jesus Christ, Son of God." The second part of the prayer is the supplication, our request to God: "have mercy on me, a sinner." The structure and words of the prayer may seem uninviting to some people. Some people have difficulty connecting to God through Jesus. Others may have problems with using the word *sinner*, finding the connotations too negative. Since the purpose of the prayer is to find that deep connection with God within, we can modify the prayer to make it more meaningful to each of us without losing the underlying power of the prayer. For those uncomfortable with the traditional prayer, take the two parts of the prayer as a model and design your own prayer. The power of the Jesus Prayer is that it is meant to bring us to that central place inside, where we touch the divine nature in all of us, the place where our authentic swing resides.

As you begin to design your own prayer, first think of the address. How do you address God? Is God "the Almighty," "my Creator," "My Father," "My Mother"? What comes to mind first when you think of God? Don't ponder this too long; just let the words come up from inside. Next, think about the supplication. What you're searching for here is the prayer that is so deep inside of you that you pray it unconsciously. You're trying to bring this up to the surface because this is the prayer that prays you. It is your authentic swing, the very ground of your being. Take a few moments now to think about this. Don't force anything; simply meditate on this question and see what surfaces. What is the immediate prayer that comes to your mind? Don't judge yourself or think "Nah, that can't be it." Sometimes our first thought is the most genuine response.

Find a place where you can spend fifteen to twenty minutes uninterrupted to do this exercise. Find a way to address God that is natural for you. Then meditate on the first prayer that comes to your mind. Don't dismiss anything. Bring all thoughts into your mind and welcome them. Find the one that fits you best—the prayer that prays you.

When I did this exercise in my spiritual director's course, I was shocked at what came up for me. I've spent most of my life running from calls to service for God. I avoided doing *Whosoever* for years until it became apparent that it was my calling. I spent years running away from a call to be ordained and serve a congregation. I've worked diligently my whole life to duck God's call, and yet the prayer that came up for me was "Dear God, how may I serve?"

That sentence was there immediately when I cleared my mind. I laughed out loud because it was exactly what I had tried to avoid. But it's my authentic self—my authentic swing: service to God and God's children. With that as my authentic swing, who can harm me? With that knowledge, how can any attack shake my faith? How can any hurtful words penetrate my heart and capture it? They can't. I'm bulletproof!

When you discover the prayer that prays you, make it your daily meditation practice. If you don't have time to sit for fifteen or twenty minutes on a regular basis, make the prayer a constant one. Say it as you get ready for work. Say it as you drive to work. Say it as you have your daily coffee break. Say it at red lights. Say it before bed each night. Honor this prayer and how it prays you. Inhale as you address God. Exhale as you give your authentic self over to God.

As that strong connection to God grows, you will find yourself becoming calmer and more able to find peace even in stressful situations. You will become less irritated by people who work against you or call you names. Instead, when challenged, you will answer from the depths of your authentic self, and your response will always be gentle and reverent.

3

LEARNING TO LOVE
THE QUESTIONS

Religion, for me, has more to do with living in the
uncertainties, with loving questions, than with
answering them. In the end, the hole in the soul
is not filled by answers. It is healed only by deeper
questions.

—*Alan Jones*, Reimagining Christianity[1]

"If you read the Bible and come away with more answers than
questions, you haven't understood the Bible," a seminary professor of mine once said. As a young seminarian, I was crestfallen
by the comment. After all, I was taking his exegesis class to
learn some answers to my questions about the Bible. I was there
to get some weapons to use against the people that kept attacking me. I wanted him to give me the tools to get at the answers
hidden among those cryptic passages, and here he was telling me
that he would do no such thing. Instead, he would give me more
questions than answers. I considered asking the school for my
money back but trudged on with the class anyway. Little did I
know that soon I would learn to love the questions and become
leery of any answers, especially if they were neat and tidy.

My professor was adept at pointing out the contradictions
of Scripture, but instead of being afraid to admit that such contradictions existed in a book held "inerrant" by some people,
he taught us to see purpose in the contradictions. They are there
to make you think—to move you beyond simple, pat answers. If
one part of the book tells you that you're saved by faith alone
but another part tells you that works earn you grace, you have
to stop and think. If one passage is interpreted as condemning

homosexuality yet another passage declares that before God there is no male or female, you have to stop and think. You suddenly have more questions than you do answers, and you begin to expand your thinking. Some more fundamentalist believers, bent on getting more answers than questions, will seek to harmonize such passages, but they tend to harmonize in the direction they want to go anyway. Living in the questions keeps you off balance—taking into account all the evidence for or against seemingly contradictory positions. Living in the questions means you keep your options open, thus keeping both your mind and (probably most important) your heart open to the stirrings of the Spirit.

Not everyone can live in the ever-changing landscape of the questions. Many people crave certainty because it gives them a sense of security. They want to know they're following the right path. They want to know that the religious tradition they've invested their lives in is the *right* one. Many get that security by defending their faith tradition tooth and nail and condemning to eternal hell all who dare to believe differently. When they read the Bible, they read it as love letter meant just for them. They find what they like, use it to form their hard-and-fast answers, and disregard the rest, pulling out the "God's Word is inerrant" trump card if faced with any hard questions.

If fundamentalist Christians deserve any credit, it's that they understand this part of human nature better than liberal Christians do. The fundamentalist strain of Christianity is growing because our world is so off-kilter, so dangerously uncertain, that the last place you want to feel unsafe is in your faith. There you want certainty and security. Fundamentalist churches have given this certainty to their flock, mostly in the form of a literal interpretation of Scripture. Read literally, the book can be seen as God's inerrant directions to us on how to live and takes our fears away by assuring us we've found the one and only way to get to God. They're on the solid rock, and all other ground is sinking sand.

Many liberal Christians don't mind it when the sand shifts now and then—that's the opportunity they need to grow and learn and ultimately draw closer to God. It is in the tension of the questions that we cultivate our bulletproof faith. But it is the hallmark of questions and uncertainty that turns many people away from liberal Christianity. Who wants questions when you can have answers? Who wants faith-rattling doubt when you can have unquestioning belief?

It's been said that the opposite of faith is not doubt but certainty. Those who have certainty have no need for faith. Their questions are all answered, and they know they're right. Those of us who love to live in the questions, however, need faith, lots and lots of it, to make it through each new question and to continue to exist in the old ones.

The Bible Said It, So I Believe It

Those who need certainty, however, seem to zero in on the Bible. They're so certain of their beliefs, they say, because the Bible tells them they are right. Instead of seeing the Bible for what it is—a compilation of divergent writings with unique voices and perspectives that often contradict one another or contain factual or scientific errors—they see it as God's instruction book given specifically to them. They take the words literally, reading out of context and without any idea of the history of the book. With that kind of belief, the Bible soon becomes an idol—a leather-bound version of God they can have, hold, and display on their coffee tables as a sign that they have found the one and only true way to connect with God.

Such beliefs can lead to some strange ideas about the Bible. Driving around Atlanta a few years ago, I saw a battered pickup truck sporting a bumper sticker that read, "If it ain't KJV, it ain't Bible."

"Well, there go the original autographs," I chuckled to myself. Apparently those Hebrew and Greek writers had it all wrong and God had to wait around for some real infallible writers to show up in the fifteenth century. It made me want to get up beside him, honk my horn, and yell, "1611, brother!" But then I'm not even sure he'd understand a reference to the date the "real" Bible was published. For him, apparently, the Bible fell from heaven written in perfect Middle English, and that was the end of the matter.

I've also heard the King James Version referred to as "the Bible Jesus read"—an even more absurd thought if you actually take the time to consider the statement. How handy it was for Jesus to have his entire life written out for him so he could fol-low along.

"Blessed are the . . . oh, wait just one minute, it's here some-where!" Jesus says, flipping through the red-dotted English pages. "Poor in Spirit! That's it. Thank heaven I've got the KJV to back me up, because, you know, if it ain't KJV, it ain't Bible!"

Take a poll, and you'll discover that many people who believe the Bible to be the inerrant word of God have no idea what the thing says. It's doubtful that many have read it, since there is that big old "begat" speed bump pretty early on in the book. Some people believe that the Bible says such things as "The Lord helps those who help themselves." Actually, Ben Franklin said that; Scripture teaches a very different lesson: that the helpless have a special place in God's heart (Romans 5:6, 8).

Other popular phrases attributed to the Bible include Hamlet's "To thine own self be true" and the family values favorite "Spare the rod, spoil the child." While the Bible does favor disciplining children, this particular phrase is nowhere to be found, but you can't tell that to the literalists.

We can hardly be surprised that so many people hold so many erroneous beliefs about the Bible. We hand people an ancient book, written in the ancient languages of Hebrew, Aramaic, and Greek and then translated into other languages like Latin and Arabic before even making it to modern lan-guages like German and English. Then we expect them to simply understand it without giving them any history. Often they are not even encouraged to read it, instead relying on what the preacher says it says. More often than not, the slogan "The Bible said it, so I believe it" really means, "The pastor said the Bible said it, so I believe it."

When they do read it, they're not equipped to understand it. Instead of learning about the history of how the Bible was compiled and the differing contexts in which each section of it was written, they're left on their own to read the English version their church prefers and apply it literally through the filter of their modern beliefs and prejudices. Of course they're going to think the Bible condemns homosexuals, since the word, in many translations, is right there in black and white in passages like 1 Corinthians 6:9. They're never told that the biblical writers didn't have that word at their disposal; it was coined in 1869. (The Bible's authors did have other words to connote homosexuality but never used them.) They're never told that the word *homosexual* first appeared in the Revised Standard Version in 1946, in part because of cultural influences and not because of any conclusive scholarship. They're never told that the translation is a mixture of two obscure Greek words and represent a "best guess" by interpreters as to what Paul truly meant. Instead, they substitute a modern word for an ancient concept that may or may not be homosexuality as we understand it today. These intricacies of interpretation are never explored by the average Bible reader because to them, it's right there in plain, unmistakable English—God hates fags!

Taking the Bible Seriously, Not Literally

I've often said that I take the Bible too seriously to take it literally. I made this statement on an Internet message board, and a fundamentalist Christian respondent called the idea ridiculous. I suppose it would seem ridiculous to someone so accustomed to reading literally, but it's not. Anyone who seeks to take the

Bible seriously could never take it literally in its English form. Such a method of reading does violence to the text. It's easy to read our own prejudices and beliefs into the passages when we read it in our preferred English translation. It's harder to do that when we employ what the theologians call the "historical-critical" method. This form of interpretation (or *exegesis*, as the seminarians call it) puts the text back in its historical context and extrapolates from there. The first question you're trained to ask in this method is, "What did this passage mean to the original audience?" In this way, we strip ourselves of the tendency to approach the text through our modern knowledge and filters. We force ourselves to think as ancient Hebrews or early Christians whenever we read a passage. Putting the passage into its historical context can be eye-opening. We need to know what the passage meant to the original audience before we can even begin to understand what eternal truth it might convey to us today.

This method is mainly practiced in those highfalutin seminaries and generally looked down on by the average man (and it usually is a man) in the pulpit at your average church every Sunday because it would deprive him of a literal reading of the English text, where modernist bogeymen like GLBT people can be found and vilified. Being forced to understand the historical context of a passage robs literalist preachers of their biggest weapon: the ability to instill fear in their congregation by projecting their modern prejudices into the text with their literal readings.

The beauty of the historical-critical method, in my opinion, is that it sweeps away those modern prejudices and modern knowledge that we take for granted when we read the Bible. If we truly are to put ourselves in the shoes of the ancient Hebrews or the early Christians reading (or hearing) early writings that later became Scripture, we have to put aside our knowledge of things like biology, how women become pregnant, how the weather works, a round earth revolving around the sun, and much, much more. We have to put aside our knowledge of sexuality and how fluid sexual orientation can be. Only when we step outside of our own narrow prejudices and modern knowledge can we begin to understand the context of the writings. Reading this way reveals more questions than answers. We must do our homework and find out about ancient cultures and their beliefs. We must dig to find answers and discover how little we truly know about these ancient ancestors. Just trying to put a passage into context often brings more questions than answers and makes the task of bringing the truth of the passage into our modern times much more difficult. To read the Bible this way makes us learn to love the questions—to be comfortable in our uncertainty and to be leery of anything or anyone that claims to have settled all the questions once and for all.

Those who use the Bible as a weapon against GLBT people resist such interpretation strategies, preferring instead to read modern ideas and knowledge into the English text as a way to back up their beliefs and prejudices and give them that satisfaction of certainty. How a person chooses to read Scripture, in the end, reveals more about the person reading Scripture than it does about the truth of Scripture.

A Short History of the Bible

Another good inoculation against reading the Bible literally—and a great way to begin to take it seriously—is to explore the history of the Bible and how it came to be on our coffee tables and nightstands.

It's embarrassing to admit, but I was actually shocked when I learned that the Bible was not originally written in English. It's more embarrassing to admit how old I was when that knowledge came to me. What came next was anger. Why hadn't my Southern Baptist church informed me of this fact? Why didn't Sunday school teachers let me in on this knowledge? Why weren't there classes on the history of the Bible in my church? Why weren't church leaders teaching us how to interpret Scripture? Why weren't we even informed about our own faith tradition?

The answer to that question came to me in the form of my mother, who, upon my announcement that I was going to attend seminary, said, verbatim, "Why do you want to go and mess yourself up like that?"

It was then I understood that in her mind, and in the minds of many other fundamentalist Christians, asking questions about your faith only invites trouble. "You'll shipwreck your faith," my mother warned me. Asking too many questions leads to too many unanswered ones, and unanswered questions lead to uncertainty, and uncertainty leads straight to the fiery pit of hell where all the unbelieving heathens who asked too many questions always go. You're better off just believing what you've been told and keeping your questions to yourself.

I disregarded her warning as so much blind-faith hogwash. "What was wrong with questions?" I thought. "Isn't that how we find answers in the first place?" I went to seminary with eyes wide shut, not anticipating the broadside that would be Christian history. In my second semester, I could see the rocks looming ahead of my ship of faith.

"Oh, dear," I thought, "my mother was right. I'm about to shipwreck my faith!"

Learning about how we got all the doctrines, like the Trinity and the Virgin Birth, nearly did my faith in. I was incredulous that anyone would believe what the church fathers (and it was always fathers) had come up with. Blood was shed over doctrines we blithely give our allegiance to today. Lives were lost, torn apart, and people were persecuted and hounded from the faith, all for believing something different from the dictates of the authorities. The entire faith seemed ridiculous. I had more questions than answers, and I hated it. I can certainly understand why some people abandon their faith in the middle of seminary. I almost did!

It was this near faith-killing shipwreck that eventually led me to a bulletproof faith. I found that after all my neat answers about faith, Christian history, and the Bible had been demolished,

I had to reconstruct them or abandon my faith all together. My faith was stronger than my doubt, and eventually, after much prayer, study, and more prayer, I was able to rebuild my faith and learn to love the questions.

This is a hidden blessing for GLBT believers. Because we are attacked for our faith, we are forced to examine it more closely. Biblically based attacks against us can serve as our impetus to delve more deeply into these passages used against us and find out the truth behind them. It's a shame that many in the GLBT community have taken the antigay interpretations of the so-called clobber passages to heart and committed spiritual suicide. We should instead view these attacks as opportunities to increase our faith and use our questions as the very foundation on which we construct our bulletproof faith.

Developing a bulletproof faith doesn't mean we will never again have questions or doubts. Instead, having a bulletproof faith means that those questions and doubts no longer ship-wreck our faith but are welcomed as opportunities to deepen our understanding of our authentic selves.

If finding out late in life about the original languages of the Bible was embarrassing, imagine my embarrassment in seminary when I learned that for the first three hundred years or so of its life, the early church had no such thing as a Bible. Many believers think that when early Christians referred to "scriptures," they were referring to the Bible we hold today. Nothing could be further from the truth. The first gospel, Mark, was written some forty years after Jesus' crucifixion (around 70 C.E.). Matthew and Luke didn't come on the scene until about twenty years later. The latest gospel, John, was written about ten years after that, some seventy years after the crucifixion! Furthermore, it's almost certain that none of the apostles for whom the books are named actually wrote any of them.

It's true that early Christian churches used these gospels and the letters of Paul (the earliest Pauline text was 1 Thessalonians, written around 50 C.E., a couple of decades before Mark) in their worship services. It was through the use of these books that they became "Scripture." The first list of the twenty-seven books that became the New Testament we consider canonical today appeared in 367 C.E. It would be many centuries later before a general consensus was reached among Christian leaders as to which texts would make up the Bible. There were many other texts that early churches used that didn't make the canonical cut, including Gnostic gospels like Thomas and other writings such as the Acts of Paul and Thecla, which told the story of a woman apostle.

For those who base their entire belief system on the Bible, these facts can and should be disconcerting. For the first three hundred years, Christians did just fine and discerned God's will fairly effectively without a leather-bound book to consult. Instead of relying on a book or being tempted to reduce that book to an idol and worship it as a literal communication from God, they trusted the Spirit to guide them. They trusted community to point them toward God. More important, they trusted their own experiences of God, through Christ and the Holy Spirit, to guide them in their lives. They didn't need a literal Bible written by impossibly infallible people to connect them to God.

For those who wish to return to the roots of the early church, the first task is to understand that the only Scripture our forebears had were the Hebrew scriptures. Their main tools for reaching God were such old-fashioned ideas as prayer, discernment, community, and experience. Furthermore, the Bible is not and was never intended as a handbook for how to live each moment. Rather it is a book of stories, recounting how other people have experienced God. When I say the Bible is a book of "stories," that is not to imply that the Bible is not true; it is. What makes them "stories" is that many of them may not be factual, but that does not diminish the underlying, eternal truth about God and God's nature revealed in Scripture. The Bible writers were not writing rules for eternity; they were simply telling the truth of how they experienced the living God. We may not agree or even identify with some of the stories, like a warrior God, but other stories may resonate with us, like God being described as a mother hen or commanding us to care for the poor and disenfranchised.

"More than anything else then," wrote Paul Alan Laughlin in *Remedial Christianity*,

> it puts the reader in touch with her or his own spirituality on the experiential level; and this, one might say, is the fundamental dynamic and true value of the Christian—or any—faith. Had the Bible been single-minded, definitive and utterly consistent, it might have stifled spiritual search and growth. As it is, however, it calls and challenges the reader to forge a living, growing, active and uniquely personal faith. At the same time, it comforts the reverent seeker with the examples of biblical authors, whose words fashioned not a flawless vessel to contain God, but a window that provides salutary glimpses of divinity, despite its surface imperfections.[2]

In short, Scripture isn't there to give us ready and pat answers to all our questions. It's there to encourage us to ask hard questions—to seek, to search, to learn how to know God through our own unique experiences. The common truths of the experiences are eternal, even if the particulars of the experiences differ from person to person.

The Authority of the Bible

The heart of the battle between fundamentalist Christians and their liberal counterparts is the question of the authority of the Bible. For our more fundamentalist brothers and sisters, the Bible has final authority. Whatever contradicts Scripture is anathema to any "true" Christian. For liberals, the Bible is *among* the authorities Christians must consult when facing tough decisions. Other things can come into play—experience, reason, and yes, even tradition. Fundamentalists may take these other things into account, but when it comes down to brass tacks, the Bible trumps them all. For liberals, however, such things as reason and experience can trump both Bible and tradition.

This differing take on authority between the two more extreme camps of Christianity is best illustrated in the case of the acceptance of gay, lesbian, bisexual, and transgender people not just in society but especially within the church. We are warned that if we accept GLBT people, the whole truth of the Bible is negated. What that argument misses, however, is that we as Christians have disregarded many things the Bible speaks approvingly of, including polygamy, subjugation of women, division of the races, and slavery—and we've done it without compromising the ultimate authority of the Bible. We read approval of these things in the Bible as cultural mores we no longer hold. Even the most strident literalist will not take the admonition to put adulterers to death as a rule we should enforce today. That same literalist may also be divorced for some other reason than Jesus' admonition that divorce was permissible only if the wife was unfaithful. So even the most hardcore literalist among us would have to admit that the literal "word of God" has room for mercy for adulterers and men who divorce their wives for some reason other than *her* infidelity—a violation of Jesus' direct command.

So the issue of authority becomes rather sticky for those who wish to use the Bible strictly against the GLBT community. To do so, they have to disregard the many things that they've already decided the Bible is wrong about. Moving forward with the acceptance of the GLBT community does no violence to the integrity of the Bible. Denying rights to an entire class of people based on a certain interpretation of Scripture does, however, as those of different races and different genders can certainly attest to. Far from damaging the authority of the Bible, acceptance of GLBT people in society and in the church would actually strengthen the integrity and authority of the text because it would prove that God is still alive, still speaking, still able to do a new thing through the Holy Spirit moving in and through God's willing, seeking, and questioning servants.

It is the scriptures themselves that reveal God telling us, "Behold, I do a new thing! Do you not perceive it?" (Isaiah 43:19). Those who cannot perceive God doing new, startling, and wonderful things are those who cling to the letter of the law of the Bible while quashing the spirit of the words. If God is still alive and still speaking, God will speak new things to us—things not recorded in books, ancient or otherwise. Some of the new things that God has spoken to us since the scriptures were penned include monogamous relationships, the ability to eat pork and shrimp, the ability to lend money at interest, freedom for slaves, freedom for women, and freedom for GLBT people.

Jesus even showed us that we must be open to God relating to us in new and unfamiliar—yes, even uncomfortable—ways. He spent his entire ministry showing us that God does not want us to follow old, soul-killing laws, but instead, Jesus showed us new ways to reinterpret the scriptures. In Matthew 5, Jesus repeatedly said, "You have heard it said—but I say to you . . ." What we have heard is what the scriptures (the Hebrew scriptures, remember) have to say about such things as murder, adultery, divorce, breaking oaths, exacting revenge, and treatment of our enemies. All these things are scripturally sound, but Jesus reinterprets the scriptures, turning them around and negating the old in favor of the new.

Those who follow Jesus' example, reinterpreting the scriptures to include good news for GLBT people, get accused of twisting God's words—and the Pharisees, too, accused Jesus of the same thing. They were convinced of the authority of their interpretation of the scriptures and could not tolerate some itinerant preacher telling the people that God could say something new. The literalist Pharisees of our day do the same, accusing those who speak a new word in the Spirit of twisting Scripture for their own ends. They deny that God could say anything new.

If God cannot say new things, then God is as dead the trees on which the words of the Bible are written. Even the scriptures testify against such a thing. God is always doing new things, including opening wide the gates of the kingdom to GLBT people, just as they were created. The eternal question then becomes, do we perceive it?

Spiritual Survival Tips

1. Take the Bible seriously but not literally. Learn all you can about the history and interpretation of the Bible. Knowing all you can about the Bible is your best defense against those who would use it against you.

2. Do not be afraid of the questions that arise as you study the Bible. Questions are opportunities to begin building your bulletproof faith.

3. Do not think that having a bulletproof faith means that you will never have any more questions to explore. A bulletproof faith can withstand questions and uncertainty and is not afraid to explore them and come to new conclusions.

4. Learn to the love the questions. It is in the tension of the questions that we cultivate our authentic self and become truly bulletproof.

5. Do not be afraid of the Bible. It is not our enemy. I contend that even if the Bible does condemn homosexuality, we are free to disregard its prohibitions based on our modern knowledge and experience. Our society has long disregarded many ancient prohibitions of the Bible and outlawed other things it explicitly condones, like slavery.

4

WISDOM BEFORE WEAPONS

It's wisdom before weapons, Gabrielle. The moment
you pick up a weapon, you become a target.
—*Xena, on TV's* Xena: Warrior Princess,
in the episode "Dreamworker"

As I noted earlier, when I first started receiving hate mail, it affected me physically. Who were these people to tell me that God hated me and would spit me out? Who were these people to judge my faith? Who were these people who thought I'd never heard of Leviticus or Romans or 1 Corinthians? Did they believe I'd read their e-mail and think, "Wow, I must have missed those passages. I'll take *Whosoever* down immediately!" The arrogance and sheer insolence of these people amazed me and put me into a tailspin.

I would respond with every ounce of my discomfort. I wrote scathing replies, sardonic replies, sarcastic replies, or just plain mean-spirited replies. I could really dish it out. I was right, they were wrong, end of discussion! I didn't care where they were coming from. I wanted them to know my view and to know that it was right!

Marianne Williamson, in *A Return to Love*, asks the question "Do you prefer to be right or happy?" We all want to feel like what we believe is right, and when we're challenged, our natural response is to defend our beliefs—often with tooth and nail. But as Williamson points out, "God doesn't need us to police the universe." Instead of "shaking our finger" at those we believe are wrong, a better response, Williamson notes, is one of compassion and forgiveness. When we approach another person with gentleness and reverence, we do not put the person on the defensive but instead open a path to dialogue. As Williamson says, we must fight against our own ego that demands to be validated as "right." "I spent years as an angry left-winger," she notes, "before I realized that an angry generation can't bring peace. Everything we do is infused with the energy with which we do it. As Gandhi said, 'We must be the change.' What the ego doesn't want us to see is that the guns we need to get rid of first are the guns in our own heads."[1]

Of course, our first impulse is to defend ourselves—often forcefully—when we've been attacked. We want the other person to understand our perspective, to hear our arguments. But most of our attackers have no interest in hearing it. They don't want a reasoned argument. They want to tell you their opinion—which they'll claim is not their opinion, of course, but what *God says*—and have no interest in hearing yours.

This is an important question for us to ponder, however: "Do you prefer to be right or happy?" Those who constantly argue with us have made their choice—they prefer to be right. They will argue until they are exhausted. They will launch legislative drives to curb GLBT rights. They will work tirelessly in their churches to ensure that GLBT people are never ordained, accepted in leadership positions, or seated in the pews. This is what happens when we want to be right. Our lives are consumed with fighting what we hate. We constantly tie ourselves to things that make us miserable.

We must make a choice. Can we stop arguing, let go of our need to convince others that we are right, and learn to be happy instead? A friend of mine once counseled a couple experiencing trouble in their relationship. The man insisted he was right. He was so wrapped up in being right, he could not hear his wife's expressions of pain or need. My friend, frustrated after several attempts to help them, finally told the man, "You can be right, or you can be in relationship."

This is our choice. Do we want to be right—to have our views validated by those who oppose us—or do we want to seek deeper relationship with those who may be considered our enemies? Do we want to bridge the gap and find common ground, or do we simply want to be acknowledged as right by our opponents, knowing full well that many of them would rather die than give us an inch?

My oldest sister and I practice this principle of being happy instead of right. She disdains homosexuality and believes I am not living the life God would will for me. We understand each other's point of view, and we know that we cannot change each other's mind. I could spend all my time with her trying to convince her that I'm right and she's wrong—but what a miserable time we'd have together. Instead, we've opted for relationship. We enjoy our time together. We love each other and want to spend time together. So we put aside our need to be right. We choose relationship.

This is not to say that we in the GLBT community must go back into the closet or keep our lives quiet. We must still work for equality in church and society. But we do need to try our best to find common ground with those we seek as dialogue partners. This is not easy, because we want desperately to be right. We often need our views validated by others, or else we question our conclusions. When we are bulletproof, however, we can let go of the need to be right. We can choose to be happy instead.

Xena's Defense Theory

If we truly want to see a change in our opponents, we first have to be, as Gandhi said, the change we wish to see. If we wish to see our opponents respond to us in a gentle and reverent manner, we must first respond to them in a gentle and reverent manner. If we seek relationship instead of being right, we must take the first steps toward relationship. We need to learn how to speak in a way that will be heard instead of our words causing barriers to go up and ears to close. We need to learn how to truly listen to our opponents and open our hearts to them.

We must resist the urge to draw our sharp weapons of sarcasm, anger, fear, or loathing when we're attacked. Xena, the Warrior Princess, was renowned in the television series for her fighting skills, but she was always reluctant to teach them to her gentle sidekick, Gabrielle, as the following scene illustrates:

Xena: Don't confuse defending yourself with using a weapon. When you pull a sword, you have to be ready to kill. People are too quick to go for their swords. It should always be the last resort.

Gabrielle: I don't want to learn to kill. I want to learn to survive.

Xena: All right, the rules of survival. Number one: if you can run, run. Number two: if you can't run, surrender, then run. Number three: if you're outnumbered, let them fight each other while you run. Number four: . . .

Gabrielle: Wait—more running?

Xena: No, four is where you talk your way out of it, and I know you can do that. It's wisdom before weapons, Gabrielle. The moment you pick up a weapon, you become a target.[2]

Wisdom before weapons. Xena's defense theory is one where words take precedence, but as we well know, words are powerful and can be just as deadly as swords.

A classic Sufi story tells of a master who has come to a village and is asked to heal a child. The villagers crowd around, and he says a few simple prayers and tells the people, "Now he will be well." Someone who didn't believe in all this spiritual stuff said, "What do you mean? You say a few words, and the kid is supposed to get better?" The master approached the man and said, "What do mean? You know nothing of this. You are an ignorant fool!" The man becomes enraged; he turns red, his body starts to quiver, and he's about to strike out at the master when the master says, "See, if a word or two can turn you red and fill you with energy and anger, why shouldn't a few other words have the power to heal?"

Our words can create healing or suffering. It's up to us to realize this power and begin to choose our words carefully, even in response to words meant to hurt us, put us down, or denigrate us. The words we say in reply must always be gentle and full of reverence, or as Colossians 4:6 says, "Let your speech always be gracious, seasoned with salt, so that you may know how you ought to answer everyone."

But as Xena wisely pointed out, often "running away"—simply removing ourselves from the situation—may be the best thing we can do to defend ourselves. Never forget that we don't have to dignify our attackers with a response. Ever since I realized that the Delete key exists for a reason, I use it often when I receive odious e-mails. I never feel bad when I hit that key and refuse to be drawn into a fruitless debate with an enemy. Instead, I feel empowered because I know that my faith has again deflected another bullet. Running away—refusing to engage in a potentially harmful situation—is not a defeat; it is survival.

Defending Our Hope

Often, though, running away is not an option. In those situations, we need to be prepared to defend the hope that is within us; we need to rely on our inner wisdom to give the gentle and reverent response that is demanded from us by God.

The rules of spiritual self-defense are similar to the rules of physical self-defense. By studying them, we can see ways to apply them to our spiritual defense. Four aspects of physical self-defense are essential:

- Knowing that you are worth defending
- Developing the determination and confidence necessary to project capability and assertiveness

- Learning to assess and handle dangerous situations
- Understanding natural defenses and training to use them

Let's look at each aspect individually and see how it applies to developing a bulletproof faith.

Knowing That You Are Worth Defending

This is the simple yet challenging principle of loving yourself. You must know, at your very core, that you, a GLBT Christian, are worth defending. You must grow your self-esteem, accepting that you are a valued child of God.

You cannot proceed in self-defense without mastering this point. Jesus tells us to love our neighbor as ourselves, but if we do not love and value ourselves, how can we love and value our neighbor? We are also told to love our enemy. Again, if we have no love for ourselves, loving our enemy will be impossible. The only way to successfully defend yourself spiritually is to love yourself. Work on loving yourself now, forgiving yourself for things that happened in the past, and moving forward confidently.

All these things are easy to say but hard to put into practice. This I know intimately. Self-esteem has been an issue for me all of my life. My father was a Southern Baptist minister, and I was the last of five children. I inherited several things from my father: a wry sense of humor; a gift for preaching; wispy, baby-fine hair; and a horrible temper (that most often comes out in traffic). My father's rages were legendary and would probably be considered child abuse by today's definition, but in those days, it was simply a matter of not sparing the rod lest the child become spoiled. I learned quickly that the best way to avoid my father's wrath was to make myself small and as invisible as possible. If I was not in my father's line of sight during a rage, I would escape unharmed.

That was a lesson I carried into adulthood, trying my best to not draw too much attention to myself. I recall quite clearly that during my first real relationship with another woman, people would look me in the eye and ask me a question and she would answer it. I allowed her to take my power like that. I didn't have enough self-esteem to complain or even take notice that I was burying my authentic self deeper and deeper.

People who went to high school with me would probably be shocked by the revelation that I have long suffered with low self-esteem. In high school, I was the consummate nonconformist. I fell in love with Ralph Waldo Emerson in English class and took to heart his admonishment to "trust thyself: every heart vibrates to that iron string."[3] I avoided cliques, wrote scathing articles in the school newspaper about conformity, and on occasion did silly dances during pep rallies to entertain myself and those around me. But it was all pretty much an act. Bravado was my weapon because I had little wisdom. I was never a member of the in-group in school, but instead of playing the victim, I played the outcast. That didn't mean that the snubs and rejection of my peers hurt any less. It was a very painful time indeed. So in what I considered self-defense, I became the class clown, the oddball who could get a laugh out of even the most popular kids in school. That would make me feel good for a little while, but it never got me invited to parties.

My first step into healthy self-esteem was, ironically, given to me by a man who didn't like me very much. In fact, this man so wanted me to fail that he gave me a responsibility he thought would be too large for me to handle. This man was the manager of the radio station where I thought I was doing such a good job of hiding my sexual orientation. Even though we worked together for more than five years, we never liked each other. In a plot to finally oust me, he gave me an afternoon talk show. Imagine, a silly, self-esteem-deprived kid getting a talk show at a radio station that could be heard in the major market of Atlanta! It was a brilliant plan. If I failed, he got to fire me, and if I succeeded, he got to take the credit for finding a new star for the station.

I was horrified and elated all at once. Hosting the show meant I had to find guests, which meant calling complete strangers and asking them for favors. Thankfully, it's fairly easy to find people who want to be on the radio. My show was a hit, garnering fairly decent ratings in the Atlanta area. That radio show did more to help my self-esteem than anything else I could have done, and I owe it all to a sworn enemy. It's wonderful how God works sometimes.

As a lesbian, however, my self-esteem was still quite low. Even though I knew I was a lesbian by age sixteen, I remained in the closet into my twenties. It's easy to understand why: society at that time didn't take kindly to our kind, and went to great pains to instill a sense of shame in anyone who didn't feel or act heterosexual. (Arguably, society at large is becoming more tolerant toward GLBT people, but here in the Bible Belt, where I live, societal disapproval and shame still seem as strong as ever.) And if society is hostile, the church is downright dangerous. Being raised as a Southern Baptist, I knew, with every fiber of my being, that I was something God loathed. So I hid.

Like most GLBT people grappling with their sexual orientation, I also abandoned the church. I figured if God didn't like me, then I could live without God. I did fine for a while, but the situation came to a head when my then-girlfriend's sister-in-law found a love note while going through my jacket pockets. She outed us to the family, and all hell broke loose. My girlfriend's family disowned her and blamed me for turning their baby girl into a disgusting lesbian. (Little did they know that this was my first relationship with a woman but it was not hers!)

In the midst of the turmoil, my girlfriend read about a church in the Atlanta area that accepted GLBT people—the MCC. My first visit to the Metropolitan Community Church in Atlanta was amazing. For the first time in my life, I saw a clergyperson stand behind a pulpit and tell me that God loved me just as I am because that's how God had made me. I didn't need to be outed to God. God already knew that I was a lesbian because God had made me that way. God had created me as a lesbian because God thought I might enjoy it—to paraphrase

my Episcopalian friend. A journey of self-acceptance and growing self-esteem began in that church that morning, and slowly
I learned to enjoy being the lesbian God wanted me to be.

Was it an easy process? No. It required that I come to understand where to place my sense of self-worth. I spent years plac-
ing my self-worth in the hands of others: station managers,
girlfriends, churches. I located my self-esteem in relationships,
jobs, and responsibilities. I never thought to hunt for my self-
esteem within myself, rooted in that light of Christ—that
authentic self—that dwells within each of us. As Emerson
wrote, "Insist on yourself; never imitate. Your own gift you can
present every moment with the cumulative force of a whole life's
cultivation; but the adopted talent of another you have only an
extemporaneous half possession. That which each can do best,
none but his Maker can teach him."[4]

To grow our self-esteem, we must insist on ourselves and
never seek to imitate anyone. Our worth is never found outside
ourselves; it can only be found within. As GLBT people of faith,
however, we always seem to want to locate that self-esteem
somewhere out there, believing what the church has told us—
that we are mistakes or, worse, willful sinners going against
God's plan for our lives.

That low self-esteem leads many GLBT people to repress
their sexual orientation or seek out ministries that promise to
"heal" them of their homosexuality and give them a sexual identity that will be more palatable to society and the church. Both
paths lead to even lower self-esteem and often to spiritual suicide. Repression of our true sexual nature or attempts to "heal"
our God-given sexuality simply dumps more dirt over the
authentic self—that glory of God—that is meant to shine forth
in our lives with brilliance and fire. When we run away from our
sexual orientation or try to change or repress it, we no longer
trust ourselves—we give away our divine power.

If we are to have healthy self-esteem—and a bulletproof
faith—we must rely solely on our *own* experiences of God. We

must insist on the authentic self, where we each embody God. We cannot adopt the self of another person, no matter how admirable the person may be. Only our own experiences, cultivated over our entire lives, can give us the self-esteem we need to become bulletproof. Only when we trust in our own experiences of God, even if they contradict the experiences of others, will we finally live fully in the glory God intends for us.

That brings up the question of how much trust we should place in our own experience, especially if it goes against what the church has taught for centuries on topics like homosexuality. In seminary, I learned about John Wesley's "quadrilateral," the "four-legged stool" of theology: Scripture, tradition, reason, and experience. In this model, Scripture, tradition, and reason are valued above experience. Some strains of Protestantism even have a "three-legged stool," where experience is thrown right out the window—valuing Scripture and tradition more than reason. Experience is always the redheaded stepchild of theologians. It is looked down on as the weakest form of "proof" that God has moved or spoken, even though in Acts it is Peter's direct experience of God that leads him to violate Scripture and include the Gentiles in God's grace. (We'll explore this event in depth later on.)

Our experience of God is our most important guide to how we reveal our authentic self. Those experiences, indeed, are our authentic self vying for our attention, trying to be heard over the din of societal, familial, and church disapproval. We feel horrible when we give in to the pressure to be "normal" as defined by society, family, and church because we know, in our gut, that it goes against who God created us to be. But we try so hard to please—to make others happy, we make ourselves small and invisible and thereby avoid the ire of society, family, and church.

Deep within our souls, we know the truth: we are just as God created us, regardless of our sexual orientation or gender identity. No matter what society, the church, or our family has said in the past or will say in the future, our experience of God, that reassurance from God that we are loved just as we are, is all that matters.

Emerson wrote in "The Over-Soul" that "the soul is the perceiver and revealer of truth. We know truth when we see it, let skeptic and scoffer say what they choose. Foolish people ask you, when you have spoken what they do not wish to hear, 'How do you know it is truth, and not an error of your own?' We know truth when we see it, from opinion, as we know when we are awake that we are awake."[5]

We know the truth. We know it so thoroughly, we can taste it and smell it. Our authentic self knows that when anyone discounts our faith or seeks to make us feel bad simply because of our sexual identity, they are not telling the truth. We know it as surely as we know that we are awake. We also know that this wisdom comes from heaven because it is "pure, then peaceable, gentle, open to reason, full of mercy and good fruits, impartial and sincere" (James 3:17, ESV). This is the scriptural measure that we have for any experience of God.

Those who protest us, yell at us, or seek to inform us that God hates us for being gay, lesbian, bisexual, or transgender are perpetuating a lie. They are ignoring the wisdom of heaven when they are harsh with us, will not reason with us, and refuse to show us mercy. John Eldredge gives us "a bottom line test to expose the Religious Spirit: if it doesn't bring freedom and it doesn't bring life, it's not Christianity. If it doesn't restore the image of God and rejoice in the heart, it's not Christianity."[6] I would say that's true about any religion, not just Christianity. If it doesn't bring freedom and life, it is not divine.

We will grow our self-esteem and develop a bulletproof faith when we reach a place where we can reject anything that does not bring freedom and life—even if what we reject has been a doctrine or teaching of the church for centuries. As the poet John Greenleaf Whittier once remarked, "Better heresy of doctrine than heresy of heart."[7] Never betray your heart, your authentic self, because when you do, you betray your experience of God. Our hearts are good, created by a loving God who knows us intimately. You are a child of God and worth defending.

Developing Determination and Confidence

This is where we can express our zealousness for what is right. It is right and good to swing wide the gates of heaven for everyone, the GLBT Christian, as well as the legalistic Christian who tries to shut the gate on us!

We must be assertive, zealous, in our defense. We must exude confidence. We must make it known that God works in our lives every day. Anything else shows a weakness in faith, and weak faith makes us an easy mark.

The best way to project capability and assertiveness is by keeping calm in the face of adversity. We must do this by mastering our anger. Assaults on our spirituality are certain to make us mad. Our attackers have no right to question our sincerity or our motives. When they do, they make us mad.

Responding in anger only reveals your interior doubt. Remind yourself that getting angry won't fix anything. It won't make you feel better (and may actually make you feel worse). Every time I responded with anger to an attack on my faith, I felt rotten. I came away questioning. I wondered if my attacker was right! When I could calmly assess the situation, I came to realize that God loved me no matter what, but it was counterproductive to react in anger. I must learn to give a gentle and reverent response whenever my faith is attacked.

Take the time now, before an attack, to learn what makes you angry. Understand why certain things press your hot buttons. Deal with those inner issues. Learn to deal with your own internalized homophobia and anger. But remember, becoming angry with your attacker is the surest way to show the weakness of your conviction, no matter how justified your anger may be.

Learning to manage your anger can be a lifelong endeavor. I'm still working on it. Sometimes I slip and let loose when I shouldn't. I'm immediately sorry, but I have to continue to work at it, every single day. Don't be discouraged if your journey to a bulletproof faith is not linear. We all stumble along the path.

Learning to Assess and Handle Dangerous Situations

In physical self-defense, this warning is usually meant to keep you from putting yourself in harm's way. By learning to recognize dangerous situations, you can learn to avoid them. This can certainly come in handy as we develop a bulletproof faith. No one is encouraging you to look for fights or to start unnecessary arguments. It's smart to pick your battles wisely, if you can.

Often, however, we cannot avoid dangerous situations. They can sneak up on us when they're least expected. That's why we must learn in advance how to assess and handle them when they do crop up. It's necessary at this stage to learn how to handle fear. When a challenge arises, we are fearful for the hopefulness that is within us. We are afraid we will lose that hopefulness or that our attacker will have the power to take it from us.

We need to stop now, before an attack comes our way, and examine the source of our fear. For me, it was the fear of being wrong. I had been taught many things about the Bible, and coming out as a lesbian challenged a majority of those beliefs. I found out that I had to rethink many of the things I had been taught about God. Many GLBT people in my position simply abandon their faith when they hear from people they have respected in the past that God will not love them if they embrace their sexuality or gender identity.

Those of us who remain engaged in the faith work from a place of often paralyzing fear. When I first encountered scholarly writings explaining that the Bible did not condemn GLBT people, my first thought was, "They're twisting Scripture!" Because of the beliefs that I had held since childhood, the interpretations of gay-friendly scholars sounded all wrong to me. My fear began to rise. If my beliefs about how God felt about GLBT people had been wrong, then what else about my faith could be wrong?

The core problem is that I believed I had the truth—until I was faced with something that other people believed to be the truth. Their belief was just as deep and just as sincere as my own, and I had several choices: I could deal with the contradictions, give up my faith, or simply retreat back into my long-held beliefs and repress my sexuality.

We are not alone. It's easy to believe that our faith is the one true faith and fight against anyone else who holds a different belief. In the children's book *Old Turtle and the Broken Truth*, Douglas Wood tells a powerful story about how we cling to our own idea of truth and battle anyone who believes differently from us. The book tells of a beautiful stone that fell from the sky. Before it hit the ground, it split in two, with the pieces falling far apart. A man discovers half of the stone and takes it back to his people. Etched on the stone are the words "You are loved." The people take this to mean that only they are loved, and they grow suspicious of the peoples and nations around them who are different from them and hold different beliefs. They launch wars on the others to defend their truth.

One day, a little girl travels to the place where the stone was found. There she encounters Old Turtle, a wise being who tells her that the stone her people have discovered was broken, and he helps her find the missing piece. She brings it back to her people, who resist her. They cannot understand what she is trying to tell them until her piece is joined with piece they already have. When reassembled, the stone reveals new words. The whole inscription now reads "You are loved, and so are they."

Whenever we feel that our beliefs may be wrong, we must understand that none of us possesses the whole truth. We see through a mirror darkly on this side of eternity, and we need each other to arrive at the place where we understand that we are loved but so are they—and "they" are anyone who may challenge our truth or make us feel fearful.

As Old Turtle tells the little girl, "The broken truth, and life itself, will be mended only when one person meets another—someone from a different place or with a different face—and sees and hears . . . herself. Only then will the people know that every person, every being is important, and that the world was made for each of us."[8]

If we are so fearful about having the foundations of our faith shaken by new ideas about God, it's not hard to imagine that our attackers may be feeling that same kind of fear. They, too, have been told that GLBT people are an abomination before God. To meet a GLBT person of faith who challenges that truth can produce the same kind of fear we may have felt when we were seeking to reconcile our sexuality and spirituality.

If we are aware of the source of our own fear, we are less susceptible to giving in to that fear when we are faced with people who criticize our faith. If we understand that we are loved, but so are they, we can realize there is no need to fear our attackers because they too are beloved children of God simply looking to heal their own broken truth.

Understanding Natural Defenses and Training to Use Them Effectively

The best antidote for fear is love, since "perfect love casts out fear" (1 John 4:18). Of faith, hope, and love, the greatest of these is love. Ultimately love soothes our anger. Ultimately love casts out fear. Ultimately love defends our hope. Learn to love, and you will make your faith bulletproof.

But what is love, and how can we train to use it effectively?

Let us begin by looking at the word *love*. What kind of love are we talking about? Is it the warm fuzzies you feel for your dog?

Is it the erotic love you feel for your partner—that *eros* kind of love? Is it the love of companionship you feel for your closest friend—that *philia* kind of love? It is none of these. Love of neighbor is an attitude, purely under control of the will. This is what is known as *agape* love. This is a love of compassion, benevolence, and goodwill. We are called to love, even if we don't like.

Martin Luther King Jr. said we should be happy Jesus did not command us to like our enemies: "*Like* is a sentimental and affectionate word. How can we be affectionate toward a person whose avowed aim is to crush our very being and place innumerable stumbling blocks in our path? . . . That is impossible. But Jesus recognized that love is greater than like. When Jesus bids us to love our enemies, he is speaking neither of eros nor philia; he is speaking of agape, understanding and creative, redemptive goodwill for all men."[9]

Paul defines this agape love in 1 Corinthians 13:4–8: "Love is patient and kind; love is not jealous or boastful; it is not arrogant or rude. Love does not insist on its own way; it is not irritable or resentful; it does not rejoice at wrong, but rejoices in the right. Love bears all things, believes all things, hopes all things, endures all things. Love never ends."

Christian love takes no joy in condemning others to hell. In our Christian love, we do not demand our own way. We seek relationship instead of being right. In our Christian love, we do not boast that we have the only way to God. We are not arrogant enough to think our beliefs are right and all others are wrong. Christian love is not irritable or resentful. We do not resent those who do not believe as we do. We do not become irritable with their opinions. No, in Christian love, we bear all things, we hope all things, and we endure all things, because love is eternal!

How on earth can we do all this? We certainly cannot do it by ourselves. God is the only one who can help us love in this way. Left to our own emotions and motives, we could never love anyone like this, not even ourselves! We must seek God's strength on a daily, maybe even hourly basis to love others in this fashion. It is hard for me to love many fundamentalist Christians in this way when I know that some have worked to continue discrimination and oppression of GLBT persons. But I am commanded to love them. With God's help, I can develop an attitude of love toward people different from myself. We must maintain a loving attitude, even if we don't feel any love.

However, feelings are an integral part of our love of neighbor. Empathy, sorrow, and anger can be feelings prompted from love. I feel all of these when I think of fundamentalist Christian leaders. I empathize with their mission of bringing God to people, I sorrow when they miss the point of unconditional love, and I get angry when they try to marginalize me and shut the gates of heaven on me because I'm a lesbian. But my feelings all spring from the love I have for their ultimate well-being. That is why the other feelings are so real, because these actions deeply injure my sense of love.

Consider the example of Jesus. He did some very radical things. He upset tables of money-changers in the temple, he blasted the scribes and the Pharisees of the day, he rebuked, he disapproved—he did it all out of love. He was (and still is) trying to shake humanity out of its unloving, selfish state. Sometimes he had to use extreme measures and extreme words (take, for example, the passage where Jesus warns that anger against a brother or sister is on par with committing murder; Matthew 5:21–22). These radical statements and actions are designed to shake us from our complacency so that we can learn to love God with all our heart, mind, and soul and to love our neighbors as we love ourselves.

Once we shake that complacency, we can look to Mahatma Gandhi to take us one step further on the road to genuine

Christian love. Gandhi not only encouraged us to love our enemies but also to try to understand them and engage them in dialogue. Both Mahatma Gandhi and Martin Luther King Jr. emphasized that the ultimate goal is not to "defeat" our oppressor but to make him our ally and friend. Jesus would agree. In Matthew 5:25, he tells us to "make friends quickly with your accuser." Gandhi's "soul force" principles offer us a way to do that. They may be hard to take at first, but we must strive to learn and implement them as GLBT Christians:

> I believe that my opponent, too, is a child of God and that we are members of one human family. I believe that my opponent is not my enemy but a victim of misinformation, as I have been. I believe that my opponent's motives are as pure as mine and of no relevance to our discussion. I believe that even my worst opponent has an amazing potential for positive change. I believe that my opponent may have an insight into truth that I do not have. I believe that one day, my opponent and I will understand each other and that if we conduct our mutual search for truth guided by the principles of love, we will find a new position that will satisfy us both."[10]

These principles do require that your opponent be willing to have a serious dialogue with you. But often the people who are attacking you are not interested in dialogue. They want to prove that they are right and you are wrong. They will try every trick in the book. They'll call you names. They'll condemn you to hell. Most of all, they will disbelieve your sincerity. The only thing you can do in this situation is respond in love. Choose to be happy instead of right.

By responding in love, you will have sufficiently defended the hope that is within you. You will have taken careful measures to handle your anger and your fear. You will have taken time to cultivate a mind of love and to create an inner tranquillity in God that no attack can disturb. You will have developed a tough mind and a tender heart, knowing that it's always wisdom before weapons.

Spiritual Survival Tips

1. Give up your need to be right. Instead, seek to be in relationship with those who oppose you. Stop engaging in pointless and frustrating arguments over whose view is "right."

2. When you are attacked, do not respond in kind. Do not use words as weapons, for if you do, as Xena said, you must be prepared to kill. Instead, your response should always be gentle and reverent. Be the change you wish to see.

3. Trust your experience of God, even if it goes against what the church teaches. Even Jesus went against traditional teaching when he expressed his experience of God.

4. Don't engage in any arguments about your faith. Running away—refusing to be drawn into a potentially harmful situation—is not a defeat; it is survival.

5. Love yourself, and understand that you are worth defending. Until you do this, you will never be able to truly love your enemies.

6. Learn to master your anger. Develop the determination and confidence you need to project capability and assertiveness in case of an attack on your faith.

7. Learn how to assess and handle dangerous situations so that you can overcome your fear. Remember that your attackers are probably working from a feeling of fear as well—a fear that what they believe about GLBT people is wrong.

8. Understand that your natural defense is love, and train to use it effectively by loving people as they are, not as you wish them to be.

SPIRITUAL SURVIVAL EXERCISE: SURRENDER BEFORE BATTLE

In the next chapter, we will discuss some of the weapons available to us when we find ourselves in potentially harmful situations that we cannot avoid. Before we begin our weapons training—before we step into battle—there is one thing we must do: surrender. That may seem strange—surrendering before the fight—but if we are to become truly bulletproof, we must surrender our whole lives, our whole spirit, our whole will to our Creator. It is only through our entire surrender that we will be able to discover our authentic self and defend our hope with honesty, gentleness, reverence, and agape love.

During one particularly traumatic time in my life when my partner and I hit a rough patch in our relationship, I learned the value of total surrender to God. It was a painful time, fraught with worry and sorrow. It was so painful, in fact, that it affected me physically. Most days I had to have a chiropractor or a massage therapist work out the knots that all the stress of the situation had manifested in my body. I had joined a small meditation group at that point, and during one particular session, for whatever reason, I simply gave it all up. I gave up my worry, my pain, my grief, my sorrow, my anger, my frustration. I surrendered totally to God in an honest and heart-wrenching prayer.

In that moment of total surrender, I felt a certain warmth—not the heat of a furnace but the warmth of a blanket being wrapped around me. I could feel the warmth flow throughout my body. It also felt as though arms were encircling me in a close embrace. Then I heard, just as clearly as someone whispering in my ear, "You will be safe. You will be loved. You will be provided for." Tears began to roll down my cheeks as I realized that God had come into my little space. God's arms were wrapped around me, filling me with warmth and comfort in a time of total surrender.

I now know how the paraplegic must have felt when Jesus told him to take up his mat and walk. I had been paralyzed by my fear, anger, and anguish. It was wreaking havoc on my body, spirit, and mind. But no more! I arose from my meditation a stronger, more centered, and happier person. Did the situation immediately resolve? No. It was still months before my partner and I would be able to reconcile our relationship, but the surrender made me bulletproof. The assurance of God manifesting in my authentic self, God walking beside me, above me, below me, and in and through me, gave me the strength and the stamina to make it through until the situation did resolve.

Now is the time to surrender yourself to God—before a battle comes your way. Now is the time to let go of anything that is bothering you, to let God take control over those areas of your life that seem hopeless. Take the time to do this short meditation, and let go of whatever it is that has you paralyzed in fear, grief, or anguish.

Find a comfortable spot where you will not be interrupted for the next fifteen to twenty minutes. You can sit or lie on the floor, on a mat, or in a chair, but it's important to remain alert during the entire meditation. Begin by following your breath: notice the tempo of your breathing—don't force it, just notice your regular breathing and fall into its natural rhythm. Don't worry if you mind wanders; that's natural. Just call your mind back to following your breath each time you notice that you have strayed. Be patient with yourself, and return to your breath as often as you need to. When you have successfully followed your breath for a few rounds, begin your prayer. Here is a prayer you can use that is specific to developing a bulletproof faith when you are attacked for your sexual orientation or gender identity, but feel free to pray what's in your own heart:

> Wonderful God, thank you for this time when I can come to you. I know that you are here for me. Lord, my heart is heavy with grief, despair, and anguish. I feel attacked from all sides. The church, my family, my society, they all tell me that you don't love me, that there is something wrong with me. God, this is causing me to feel hopeless. I don't know what to say to them. I don't know how to tell them that all my experiences of you have led me to believe that I am right with you, that I am made in your image and you have made me as I am. Lord, you know my deepest heart, for that is where you dwell in me. There is nothing about me that you do not know, no hidden secrets, no dark places. Your light shines in every part of my soul.
>
> Lord, I come to you now, ready to surrender all to you. I ask that you lift this burden from my shoulders—take away the pain and anguish that it has caused me. I give to you now all my fear, all my pain, all my sorrow, all my grief, all my despair, all my anger, all my hopelessness, all my agony. [Tell God about any other feelings or emotions that are bothering you.] I am paralyzed by these feelings, God. I ask for your healing touch so that I may take up my mat and walk—free from these emotions that have held me hostage.
>
> As you take these crippling emotions from me, God, I ask that you replace them with your strength, your courage, your joy, and your peace. Give me the words I need when I need them. Give me the resources I need to grow my faith, to become bulletproof in the face of persecution or attack. I invite you now to manifest yourself in my deepest heart, in my authentic self. Come forth in every area of my life with the force of your Spirit. Give me the strength and courage I need to face every battle with confidence. I surrender all to you, knowing that in my full surrender comes complete victory in and through your mercy and grace. Amen.

After you have finished your prayer, return to your breath. A short mantra may help you stay with your breath. Repeating a phrase like "God, be with me" or "Lord, have mercy" as you breathe in and out can help you stay with your breath. Continue following your breath or using your mantra until the full fifteen or twenty minutes have passed.

I cannot guarantee you will have the same experience of God I did using this meditation. I am, however, absolutely sure that when you fully and honestly surrender yourself to God, you will no longer be paralyzed by the emotions that keep you from living as your authentic self. You cannot fake God out. You can sit for hours in meditation and not feel a thing if you're just trying to convince God you're really surrendering when you have no intention of complete surrender. Only when you truly let go of the emotions that paralyze you will you feel God's peace wash over you. It may feel different from my experience, but trust me, you will know God's presence in that moment. In whatever way God needs to speak to you, God will. It will be unmistakable. And it will be beautiful.

5

LEARNING THE OUTWARD MOVES

Refuse to get involved in inane discussions; they
always end up in fights. God's servant must not be
argumentative, but a gentle listener and a teacher
who keeps cool.

—*2 Timothy 2:23–25* (The Message)

Now that you have surrendered—you're ready for battle. Remember, Xena did not leave Gabrielle completely defenseless. Even though dialogue and running away are viable options, Gabrielle was still very skillful with a staff. She did know the outward moves she needed to defend herself physically, if it came to that. Thugs didn't want to mess with Gabrielle—she was bulletproof—well, swordproof, at least.

Until now, we've mainly been talking about how to defend ourselves from people who send hate mail to us or say hateful things to us. For these kinds of attacks, Xena's advice to run away—or simply walk away—is the wisest. Such attacks do not warrant any sort of serious response; that's not what the attackers are looking for. These attacks are verbal hit-and-runs: the attackers are not interested in holding a conversation; they want to have their say and move on. I can't count the number of times I've received e-mails with fake return addresses. Even if I wanted to send a gentle and reverent response, I couldn't, and that suits the attackers just fine. They don't have a bulletproof faith—they have a weak faith that needs to make itself feel better by attacking the faith of another person. These kinds of "drive-by" attacks, then, warrant no response.

However, not all people who feel that homosexuality is wrong are rabid in their opposition. There are indeed some people in our faith communities who are seeking common ground with GLBT people in their midst. For these people, we must have reasoned arguments and thoughtful commentaries at the ready when our hope is challenged. We would be remiss in our training if we did not seriously seek dialogue and communion with our brothers and sisters who seek this with us. But if our first impulse is to strike out in fear, anger, or frustration at our detractors, we may not be able to discern between those seeking real dialogue and those seeking to lob hate bombs. Often these two sorts of people speak the same language initially, telling us that we're "living in sin" or using the "love the sinner, hate the sin" line. We must be able to discern between the well-meaning person who hasn't yet been educated in how to speak to us lovingly and the hateful bigot who doesn't care about speaking lovingly.

There are ways to tell these people apart when you are having a religious discussion about GLBT issues. Those who seek to attack will take every opening we provide to try to goad us into becoming angry or frustrated. Those who want dialogue with us will listen to our faith journeys. Their questions will be gentle and probing. They will be genuinely curious about our lives. Those intent on assaulting our faith have no such curiosity. They simply want to win an argument against us. Use your judgment, but be prepared to walk away from any discussion that becomes abusive. This is your best form of self-defense.

The Discussion

In discussions with people who oppose homosexuality, I have never heard anything new. They all say the same things. They all quote the same Bible verses. All the arguments against homosexuality have been made. But better yet, all those arguments against homosexuality have been refuted, so a lot of our work has already been done for us. All those arguments and their refutations can be found in books and on Web sites (see the reference list in the Recommended Reading and Online

Resources sections at the back of this book). These are the resources we must be familiar with—not so much to use during arguments but to fortify our own faith. When we are well versed in all the arguments against homosexuality and their refutations, we become bulletproof and recognize that we don't have to engage in this inane discussion. No matter what others say to us or about us, we know the truth. We know that they have bought into the lies about our lives—sometimes innocently and with good intentions—but they have bought into lies nonetheless.

Perhaps the lie that irks me the most is the repeated use of the word *lifestyle* when referring to GLBT people. Apparently, we don't have lives; we have "lifestyles." I've been told by many people that I need to change my "lifestyle." My standard response is that I'll be happy to change my "lifestyle" if they would be so kind as to contribute a few thousand dollars. After all, my lifestyle is a reflection of my income, not my sexual orientation, and if they're so concerned about it, they are welcome to contribute to the cause.

People who object to GLBT people hammer the word *lifestyle* to describe our lives because it's easier to dehumanize and dismiss us if we are just "living a lifestyle." It's easier to make the general public believe that homosexuality can be easily changed because it's simply a matter of altering one's "lifestyle"—not changing one's authentic self.

The truth is that GLBT people have lives—lives that can be full and rich if only they'll stop believing the lies themselves and instead live authentically as the GLBT person that God created them to be. Take the time now to formulate responses to critics' spurious arguments before any attacks come your way. Remember, you're not training to fight—you're training so you won't have to fight. When the protester at our church groundbreaking yelled his insults, I could have refuted everything he said—but I didn't feel the *need* to refute them. I was bulletproof—and none of my arguments would have changed his mind. Any confrontation would have simply resulted in angry words that would condemn me as much as they would condemn him. Nothing would have been accomplished.

So when we are confronted, we have many options. We can take Xena's advice and run away, or we can engage. When we choose to engage in a religious discussion with someone, we must remember to be gentle and reverent, even if the other person is not.

(At this point, I highly recommend that you go to the Fairness Project Web site at http://fairnessproject.org and order Dr. Robert Minor's booklet *When You're Having a Religious Argument*. This chapter reviews some material from that booklet, but it contains so much more that you'll want to explore.)

Here are some things to keep in mind if you choose to have a religious discussion:[1]

- Do not argue about Scripture, religious traditions, or doctrines. "Prooftext" wars—battles based on biblical passages bandied about as "proof" of one's point of view—are futile; they only lead to anger and frustration. No one wins a prooftext war. You may feel smug and superior or that you made a better argument, but in fact you botched the chance to turn an enemy into an ally.

- Make it clear that you disagree with antigay interpretations, doctrines, and institutions. Your responses should be short and straightforward, for example: "I don't agree," "I think that's wrong," or "I know that some people interpret it that way, but I don't."

Your opponent may try to draw you into a prooftext war, but don't give in—keep repeating your clear statements of disagreement without elaboration as often as necessary. If you sense that the other person is genuinely interested in hearing your point of view, express it—calmly, gently, and reverently. If true dialogue begins, you can talk further about your beliefs and try to engage the other person in a deeper conversation. But if your statements are only being used as a springboard to attack or goad you again, take Xena's advice and remove yourself from the situation. Use your judgment, but at no time should you allow anyone to vilify, taunt, or abuse you in any way because of your beliefs.

Your "Stuff" Versus Their "Stuff"

Anyone who has been in church long enough knows that there is usually one person who is particularly difficult. This is the person you don't want to be stuck sitting next to at the church potluck. It's the congregant who seems to do nothing but complain, obsess, and otherwise drive you nuts. It's all you can do to be cordial, all the while hoping that someone will come and rescue you.

I was once approached by a congregation member who asked me how to deal with a particularly difficult person. I told him that my years of experience had taught me that God continued to put difficult people in my life because what irritated me most about each one of them was often something I didn't like about myself. This was not the answer the man was looking for. In fact, it horrified him. He seemed puzzled for a few moments but then began to reflect on how similar he was in certain ways to this difficult person. Moral of this story: work out your own demons, and the perceived demons of others suddenly disappear.

This is also true about those who may attack our faith because of our sexual orientation. We react strongly to them because they arouse something in us that is yet unresolved. When we bristle at the idea that God hates homosexuals, we bristle not because of the person saying the words but because somewhere within ourselves we still believe that God hates homosexuals. We may react harshly to the person saying the words, but it's not the person that has angered us—it's our own unresolved feelings around whether God truly loves us as the GLBT person God made us to be. Put simply, when we are upset by other people's stuff, that's our stuff, and we need to go into our own heart and resolve those conflicts to develop a bulletproof faith.

When you're engaged in a religious argument or discussion, you can identify those hot buttons within you by keeping a few questions in mind:

Why does this issue or this particular argument matter to me?

What emotional need am I meeting by arguing about religion?

What prevents me from walking away or ignoring the source?

Why do I stay in a religious community that does not agree with me and wishes me to leave?

Why do I care about [this person's] beliefs, particularly if I disagree?

When do I know it's time to leave?[2]

The point here is to examine what buttons get pushed—what happens to us during an argument or attack. When we are provoked or feel anger or resentment arising in us during a religious discussion or attack, we must learn to use those feelings as a reminder that we're wandering into an area of our inner selves that has yet to be mastered. As we become more and more irritated, we should deepen our listening. In fact, if we really feel irritated and angry, that's our cue to just shut up. Nothing we say in this agitated state will help the situation. Indeed, it will only make it worse. Speaking from a place of resentment and irritation will not add peace and harmony to the world.

Resentment and anger can be useful, however. Let these emotions remind you that you should never respond to anyone unless you can do it in a gentle and reverent manner. Then, when the confrontation is over, use it as learning material. Open yourself further, and examine why your buttons got pushed and meditate on how you can deactivate those buttons forever.

It's Not Personal

The fastest way to get your buttons pushed is to take personally whatever another person says to you. This is easy when another person is questioning not just your faith but your entire existence as a child of God. It's difficult *not* to take that personally. If you want to become bulletproof, though, you must train yourself never to take anything someone else says as a personal insult.

You do this by shifting your attention from yourself to the other person. Just as we quiz ourselves on our motives for why we continue to engage in religious arguments or stay in unwelcoming churches, we must begin to question the motives of those who attack us. What is at the root of their need to argue with us about our lives and our faith? What emotional need are they meeting by attacking us? Why do they care about our beliefs? What keeps them from walking away?

Authors Philip Gulley and James Mulholland understand what it's like to be attacked for their beliefs. In their book *If Grace Is True*, they argue that God will save every person. Grace is not a limited-time offer that we must accept before we die. Instead, God's grace is infinite, and no one will miss out on redemption. No one will be committed to the flames of hell forever, not even people considered truly evil, like Hitler. "The only fire Hitler requires is the fire of divine love, which will consume the dross of his hatred and evil, leaving him humbled and repentant, and seeking his proper place in divine order," they write.[3]

Hitler in heaven? Only the thought of GLBT people in heaven could be more horrifying to fundamentalist Christians bent on condemning those they disagree with to eternal hell. Indeed, Gulley and Mulholland's words offended the fundamentalist Christian community, and their book was soundly condemned. The thought that their enemies will be reconciled with God at some point, even after their death, was simply too much for some people. Gulley and Mulholland received angry, threatening letters, and protesters showed up at their public appearances.

Gulley, speaking at a forum I attended at Guilford College in Greensboro, North Carolina, in 2003, recalled one of those people. A woman came up to him after they spoke about their book and began to tear into him about the book's premise. Gulley said that as he gazed at the woman raging before him, he didn't take anything she said personally. Instead he wondered, "What kind of pain has she experienced in her life that this book would make her so angry?"

Gulley understood that her anger wasn't about him or anything he and Mulholland believed. Instead, something in their book had sparked some sort of pain within *this person*. He understood that her rage came from *her* stuff, not his or Mulholland's. By showing this woman compassion and refusing to argue with her, Gulley was a gentle listener, a teacher who kept his cool.

I took this lesson to heart after hearing their lecture and immediately began putting it into practice. It made me bulletproof. As I walked by the shouting protester at our church groundbreaking, I couldn't help but wonder what his pain was all about. What had happened in his life that made it so important to him to make crude signs denouncing other human beings? What had happened in his life that convinced him that the only way to make himself feel better was to make others feel bad? What was his pain? Where did it come from? My heart broke for him. I still keep him in my prayers, hoping that God will heal whatever it is inside of him that remains so broken.

I had a similar experience in 2007 when I attended a Soulforce Equality Ride action at Bob Jones University in Greenville, South Carolina. I went to cover the event for *Whosoever*. The scene was amazing. On one side of the four-lane highway stood the young Soulforce protesters, staging a silent vigil against antigay student policies at the private Christian college. On the other side of the highway stood several groups of bullhorn- and sign-carrying protesters. The protesters were loud, shouting angry words of condemnation of homosexuals and homosexuality.

I spoke with several of the protesters, who assured me that the "sodomites" across the street would burn in hell. Somehow, the thought seemed to make them happy, even though they denied it. One particularly loud street preacher told me he loved the homosexuals that he was yelling at. I doubted his sincerity in light of 1 Corinthians 13, which tells us that love is "patient" and "kind" and above all is not "rude." I couldn't imagine Jesus using a bullhorn to shout down the Pharisees. Jesus used love, compassion, and understanding—just as the Soulforce protesters did that day.

As I stood across the street from the protesters, I pondered the literal and spiritual divide between us. What was their pain? What would motivate a group of people to paint signs of condemnation and speak loud, rude words against another group of human beings? What had happened in their lives that made them believe that shouting slurs and condemnations is a valid expression of love? They were certainly not gentle listeners or teachers who kept their cool.

My theory is that what motivates them is fear. I believe that their fear is most likely grounded in a genuine concern for the eternal well-being of everyone, but the fear is so overwhelming that they're not sure how to get their message across. Simply telling people the good news of the gospel doesn't seem to work, so they've resorted to shock tactics to try to shake those they believe are on the wrong path. If they truly believe that GLBT people are going to hell and they truly care about their fate, they might resort to almost any tactic to try to turn gays and lesbians from what they believe is a "lifestyle" that leads to eternal damnation. Their fear for the lives of other people may be compelled by true compassion, but their tactics have become extreme.

I believe that this overwhelming fear, born out of true compassion, can lead someone to carry an offensive sign or shout their "love" from a bullhorn. This overwhelming fear, born out of true compassion, is what can motivate a total stranger to shout at Philip Gulley or make fundamentalist Christians lash out at GLBT Christians in hysterical raves.

This understanding came to me as I read a passage from Steven Pressfield's *War of Art:* "Fundamentalism is the philosophy of the powerless, the conquered and the dispossessed. Its spawning ground is the wreckage of political and military defeat, as Hebrew fundamentalism arose during the Babylonian captivity, as Christian fundamentalism appeared in the American South during Reconstruction, as the notion of the Master Race evolved in Germany following World War I. In such desperate times, the vanquished race would perish without a doctrine that restored hope and pride."[4]

It doesn't seem true that fundamentalist Christians could still see themselves as powerless, conquered, and dispossessed. They wield much political and social power, but just ask fundamentalists who the powerless, conquered, and dispossessed are, and they'll gladly take the title for themselves. Gays and lesbians are powerful in their mind because society is coming around to accepting us—ignoring their loud protests. They are still smarting from losses over slavery and equal rights for African Americans and women. They remain bitter that interpretations of the Bible that once backed these prejudices are now rejected. They see the same thing happening to their beliefs about GLBT people, and yes, they feel powerless, conquered, and dispossessed.

Pressfield writes that the fundamentalist "can't find his way into the future, so he retreats to the past. He returns in imagination to the glory days of his race and seeks to reconstruct both them and himself in their purer, more virtuous light. He gets back to basics. To fundamentals."[5]

While I still don't totally understand the fear and pain of fundamentalist Christians and what makes them take to the streets with such venom, I find that the more I encounter them, the more my heart breaks for them—and for myself. There but for the grace of God go I.

If I had been born heterosexual, I probably would be like my two sisters, fundamentalist Christians, married to fundamentalist Christian men, raising a family and going to a fundamentalist Christian church. I would have had little reason to be otherwise. We are all a product of our circumstances. If any of those bullhorn-carrying preachers on the street in Greenville had encountered different factors in life's journey, they could have turned out completely different, too. They could be standing up for the rights of the oppressed and marginalized instead of working to further oppression and marginalization.

We must keep this in mind, or else we'll always take personally any attack that comes our way.

Heed the Warnings

Even though we work hard to be prepared for an attack, we still may get sucked into an argument about our faith and sexuality. It's important that we understand the warning signs that we're getting involved in inane discussions so we can disengage.

Here are some signs to watch for:

- *Becoming irritated, frustrated, or angry.* This is a good sign that we've been completely sucked into an inane argument about our faith and sexual orientation or gender identity. The moment we get angry, we've already gone too far. The only remaining option is to stop arguing and walk away. Our anger justifies the person arguing against us; indeed, making us angry was almost certainly our attacker's intent. Bigots will take our anger as evidence that our arguments are weak, and that only strengthens their desire to attack us. So if you get angry during an argument, stop arguing. A bulletproof faith can never be goaded into an angry response.

- *Becoming defensive.* It's true that our goal in developing a bulletproof faith is defense, but that's no reason become *defensive.* The moment we feel like we're being forced to justify our beliefs to someone is the moment our self-defense turns into defensiveness. Remember that you never have to justify your beliefs or your sexual orientation or gender identity to anyone. Jesus warned his disciples never to justify themselves to other human beings. God knows our hearts. God guides our faith. That's all we the approval we'll ever need.

- *Feeling the need to win the argument.* We're human. We like to feel like we've scored points or won when we're debating. We know we're trapped in an inane argument, however, when the need to win at any cost clouds our mind. We become just as irrational and angry as the person who has attacked us. At this point, no matter how many points we may score against our opponent, we've already lost, because we have abandoned our bulletproof faith.

- *No longer using gentle and reverent words.* If we find ourselves personally attacking our attacker, giving as good as we're getting, or using foul language, we've lost our way. Our discussion has devolved into a fight. Again, at this point, no one wins—feelings will be hurt on both sides. At this point, resentment grows and makes it harder for either side to see the humanity in each other.

I experienced every single one of these warning signs—and heeded none of them—when my brother-in-law confronted me over the issue of homosexuality a few years ago. He is a staunch believer that homosexuality and Christianity are incompatible. During a visit with him and my sister, he pounced, insisting that I read a pamphlet on why the Bible condemns homosexuality.

"If you think the sin of Sodom and Gomorrah was inhospitality, you need to read this," he said emphatically as he pushed the pamphlet across the table to me. I politely declined the pamphlet, pointing out that it's not just my belief that inhospitality was Sodom's sin but the Bible's as well (Ezekiel 16:49–50). This information seemed to energize him. He launched into all of the biblical arguments against homosexuality that I have heard ad nauseam. I listened as patiently as I could and calmly repeated the phrase "I don't agree," but I could feel my frustration and anger growing. Warning sign number one.

Then I got defensive. I started to justify myself. I reminded my brother-in-law who had the master's degree from an accredited seminary. I reminded him who had studied the Bible in depth. I reminded him who didn't just accept what others said about the Bible but did the historical criticism necessary to understand the text for myself. I reminded him that my experience with God was all I needed to know—not his opinion that my experiences were wrong. Warning sign number two.

I really wanted to win this argument. My brother-in-law and I used to have a great relationship. But over the years, his views about homosexuality have so consumed him that we cannot spend time in the same room now without his trying to engage me in this argument. I wanted to win once and for all, to put him in his place so that I would never have to tread this ground again. I began to try to score points—prooftexting like a pro, justifying myself with my knowledge of Scripture, letting him know that I was the smartest person in the room. Warning sign number three.

Finally, I got belligerent. My anger peaked, I was totally defensive, and I felt I had to win at all costs. I stopped using gentle and reverent language. I called him names, made rude gestures at him, and told him where he could put his opinions. Warning sign number four. Game. Set. Match.

I had lost and lost big. I wanted to be right, desperately. I wanted my brother-in-law to validate my point of view by agreeing that I was right. This is what happens when we insist on being right instead of being in relationship. If I had chosen to try to be in relationship with my brother-in-law instead of trying to be right, perhaps we could have found some common ground. Perhaps I would not have lost my temper. Perhaps he and I could have put aside our differences and related to one another in love instead of irritation and anger. Instead, I badly damaged our ability to relate to each other at all after this encounter.

I had lost the respect of my brother-in-law. That means that not just my arguments but my very life had no power to move his heart or change his mind. He'd already seen the worst of me. I'd confirmed his beliefs that GLBT people are nasty, defensive, angry people who have no valid justification for their faith. He'd seen that my faith was not bulletproof. Instead, my faith was weak because I would resort to any means necessary to defend it. A faith that needs that kind of vociferous defense is not faith but fear—the same kind of fear that drives antigay protesters to paint signs and yell into bullhorns. A bulletproof faith needs no outward defense. It is its own defense because it can withstand any attack.

When we become angry and defensive, needing to win and verbally smiting our attacker, we lose any chance to encourage real change in our opponent. I can apologize all I want to my brother-in-law, but the damage has been done. I wish I had handled it differently, but I didn't. I can't take it back. I can only hope that he meets someone better than me who can change his heart and mind on the issue of homosexuality. I blew my chance.

If I had practiced the principles of right speech, I probably could have avoided this terrible argument. I could have sought common ground with him, agreeing with him on many points but calmly telling him where we might agree to disagree. I also could have simply taken his pamphlet, thanked him, and told him that I would read it and consider it. All he really wanted was an acknowledgment that I was open to hearing him. When it became apparent that I wasn't, he tried harder and harder to reach me. If I had simply accepted his offer, I could have kept the peace, but instead of wanting to be happy, I wanted to be right, and that's where the trouble really began—with me and not with him. I know my brother-in-law well enough to realize that any discussion would be fruitless. I would not be able to change his mind. When faced with such an intractable opponent, the best strategy is to seek common ground, thank the person for being concerned, promise to think about his or her point of view, and move on. My brother-in-law and I probably could have gone on to talk about his golf game or the weather after that instead of becoming entangled in a brutal argument.

Two Steps Forward, One Step Back

As you can see, developing a bulletproof faith is not exactly a linear process. There may be setbacks—and often it feels as though you're taking two steps forward and one step back. In those moments, the best thing you can do is forgive yourself, learn from the experience, and move on. Do not beat yourself up for your failures. You'll never become bulletproof that way.

Often it's family members who trip us up most effectively. These are the people who have known us practically our whole lives, and often we feel vulnerable and defenseless around them. I have learned my lesson with my brother-in-law and will refuse to engage in these sorts of inane discussions with him in the future. It's clear that we disagree with one another, and it's clear that neither of us will change each other's mind. Arguing is fruitless and only leads to fights. Xena is my wise teacher here, and in the future, I will run away from my brother-in-law on this topic. In the meantime, I will work to deactivate the hot buttons that he uncovered in me and be grateful that he has revealed more of my "stuff" that needs work. It is this gratitude toward those who attack us that we will pick up in the next chapter.

Spiritual Survival Tips

1. Refuse to get involved in inane discussions about sexual orientation or gender identity. Repeat the phrase "I don't agree," and resist getting into prooftext wars over the Bible.

2. Remember that those who want to argue with you are dealing with their "stuff," and it has nothing to do with your "stuff." When you become upset, however, that's all about your "stuff" and not their "stuff."

3. Never take any attack personally. Remember that those who lash out against you are simply stuck in their "stuff." Act with compassion toward your attackers and the pain that has motivated them to take their fear and anger out on you.

4. Heed the warning signs that you are getting caught up in a religious argument about your sexual orientation or gender identity. Disengage from the argument at the first signs of frustration, anger, and defensiveness. Take Xena's advice and run away before you get caught using angry or hurtful words toward your opponent.

5. Do not beat yourself up if you become entangled in a religious argument. Forgive yourself, and move on. Learn from the experience, and work to deactivate the buttons the attacker pushed.

6

THE GIFT OF THE ENEMY

Love your opponents. When I say love, I don't
mean hand them the match. I mean contend with
them to the death, the way a lion battles a bear,
without mercy but with infinite respect. Never
belittle an opponent in your mind, rather build
him up, for on the plane of the Self there can be no
distinction between your being and his. Be grateful
for your opponents' excellence. Applaud their
brilliance. For the greatness of the hero is measured
by that of his adversaries.
   —*Steven Pressfield*, The Legend of Bagger Vance[1]

A traditional Zen story, circulated widely on the Internet, tells the tale of a great warrior. Though quite old, he still was able to defeat any challenger. His reputation extended far and wide throughout the land, and many students gathered to study under him.

One day, a young warrior arrived at the village, determined to be the first man to defeat the great master. Along with his strength, he had an uncanny ability to spot and exploit any weakness in an opponent. He would wait for his opponent to make the first move, thus revealing a weakness, and then would strike with merciless force and lightning speed. No one had ever lasted with him in a match beyond the first move.

Against the advice of his students, the old master gladly accepted the young warrior's challenge. As the two squared off for battle, the young warrior began to hurl insults at the old master. He threw dirt and spit in his face. For hours, he verbally assaulted the man with every curse and insult known to humankind. But the old warrior merely stood there motionless and calm. Eventually, the young warrior became exhausted. Admitting defeat, he slunk away in shame.

Somewhat disappointed that the old master did not fight the challenger, the students gathered around the old man and asked, "How could you endure such an indignity? How did you drive him away?"

"If someone comes to give you a gift and you refuse it," the master replied, "to whom does the gift belong?"

The protester at my church, my brother-in-law, and all the hate mail writers I encounter are seeking to give me a gift—the gift of insults and attack. It's my choice whether or not to accept that gift, however. A bulletproof faith refuses to accept the gift of insults and by doing so drives away its opponents. A bullet-proof faith, however, does accept, with gratitude, the *unintended* gifts that enemies bring.

Walter Wink writes in *The Powers That Be* that our enemies "can be the way to God. We cannot come to terms with our shadow except through our enemy, for we have no better access to those unacceptable parts of ourselves that need redeeming than through the mirror that our enemies hold up to us. This, then, is another, more intimate reason for loving our enemies: we are dependent on our enemies for our very individuation. We cannot be whole people without them."[2]

Instead of regarding our attackers as enemies to be defeated, those of us with a bulletproof faith see an attack as an opportunity to improve ourselves and grow stronger and more resilient. Remember, when we have issues with other people's stuff, it's really our stuff. Our enemies, then, are there to remind us of our stuff and to help us transform ourselves into better, more loving, more faithful people.

In *The Legend of Bagger Vance*, Steven Pressfield writes that if we view our opponents in this way, we soon "realize that the game is not against the foe" but against ourselves—the "little self" that we possess. "The yammering, fearful, ever-resistant self that freezes, chokes, tops, nobbles, shanks, skulls, duffs, flubs. This is the self we must defeat."³ Our attackers can serve as a constant reminder that we have yet to conquer that little yammering self that wants to respond to attacks with the same vehemence with which they are delivered. This is their gift to us. Accept it gladly.

Be Grateful for Your Enemy

The best gift I ever received from an enemy came from a man on an Internet message board that I used to frequent. He was a strict authoritarian, a misogynist, and so doctrinaire that he believed that even the most strident fundamentalist Christians were liberals. He was ruthless in his argumentation style and took particular delight in attacking anyone who talked about feelings or their personal experience of God. For him, experience was the least convincing argument anyone could make. He believed that the heart was deceitful and that feelings were merely an excuse to sin. He had spent his entire life stripping away his ability to feel, and he had done an excellent job of it. If you could not prove your argument with the Bible, he had no use for you. However, he believed that the Bible was not open to interpretation. He was fond of saying that the Bible said what it said and nothing more. There was no convincing him that by its very nature, *all* reading is interpretation, even his. In fact, the Bible as we know it comes to us from interpretation as scholars interpreted and translated ancient Greek and Hebrew manuscripts in various ways.

According to this man, however, he did not "interpret" the Bible. He read it and followed what it said, period. It was maddening! We all tried to tell him that even reading a shampoo bottle involves interpretation. By his same argument, some literalists would be stuck in the shower forever because while the bottle says, "Lather. Rinse. Repeat," it never says, "Stop." Knowing when to stop is left to personal interpretation. Despite our best appeals to logic, there was no convincing him that all acts of reading are interpretation.

So if you didn't agree with his "reading" (or interpretation) of Scripture, you were, of course, wrong. I was wrong all the time, according to this man. And wrong not just about homosexuality; I was especially wrong to think that I, as a woman, had any right even to speak about the Bible, much less proclaim myself a minister of the gospel. He was the perfect enemy I needed to become bulletproof.

I spent months going back and forth with this man. We swapped arguments, insults, and angry words. I tried every tactic I could think of: cold logic; appeals to emotion (that's when I found out the hard way that he only saw those as openings to abuse me); arguments from Scripture, reason, and tradition; and even gentle and reverent words. Absolutely nothing worked. He remained stubborn in his beliefs. He, above anyone there, had a bulletproof faith. I didn't want to have faith in what he believed in, but I certainly wanted one just as strong and impervious as his. He took apart each argument thrown at him, usually with obfuscation and outright treachery. He used a lot of double-talk and flawed logic, but nothing anyone said to him made him rethink any of his positions. His convictions were unshakable.

That is how I learned what Bagger Vance was trying to teach Junah. I never grew to like this man, but I respected him greatly. I respected him for his excellence. I applauded his brilliance. He used underhanded and dishonest tactics to "win" arguments and frustrate his opponents, but they were highly effective. Just like that old master, he refused our gifts. I certainly did not want to pattern my own faith by his, but I cherished him as an opponent.

I didn't realize how valuable this enemy had been to me until I was asked to be on a panel at a town hall meeting on same-gender marriage. The auditorium, at the University of South Carolina, was packed. The forum was held before the state ultimately passed a constitutional amendment against same-gender marriage in 2006, so the topic was hot and people were primed for debate. Each of us on the panel made opening statements about same-gender marriage, but as all of these forums go, it quickly turned into a debate about whether or not the Bible condemns homosexuality.

Questioner after questioner took to the microphones to condemn homosexuality from a biblical perspective. I saw my Internet antagonist in each of them. They all said the things that he had said. They made his same arguments, and they swore that the Bible was absolutely clear on the subject and could not be interpreted in any way but theirs.

I had an answer for them all. I'm afraid I hogged the microphone that night and barely let the other panelists tackle the questions. I answered each in a gentle and reverent manner—with confident answers grounded in the Bible, reason, and tradition. I avoided talking too much about my own experience and answered their questions clearly, in terms they would understand. One man, an African American, asserted that we should wait for opinion polls to show that the public was ready for same-gender marriage. I told him that by his own logic, if we left the granting of civil rights up to the tender mercies of the majority, he'd still be drinking from a different water fountain than me and be unable to marry a woman outside of his own race, especially in South Carolina. He saw my point.

At the end of the evening, I had many people coming up to me wanting to know how I knew all the answers to these questions. It was my Internet "enemy" who prepared me, and I knew I owed him a debt of gratitude.

Think of the maddening people in your own life. Think of all the times you've tried to argue your position with family members, church members, and even complete strangers. Instead of becoming frustrated or angry, learn to recognize the gifts they bring that you do want to accept. Their challenges make you a better, more faith-filled person. These people are your teachers. Be grateful for them. Always speak words of edification, love, and grace. We may think our opponents do some despicable things, and they certainly do, but do not ever think less of them. Do not ever be afraid to contend with them, but offer them infinite respect, even if you never receive any back. This is the key to becoming bulletproof.

Lessons from the Enemy

As I said, I learned a lot from my Internet enemy. He taught me how to hone my arguments. He taught me how to grow a thicker skin and not take things personally, and above all, he showed me places where my own issues were not yet resolved. He also served as a warning. No matter how intense our tangles got, I had to resist becoming like him—rigid, controlling, and self-loathing.

Thus we can benefit from our enemies if we stop resisting them as opponents and start embracing them as *teachers*. Let's take a closer look as some of the things I have learned from my enemies.

Exercise Self-Control

It's easy to become frustrated with those who oppose us. They insist not just that their position is right but that it is the *only* position that can be held. Certainly, we believe that our own position is right, or else there would be no argument, but if we don't have our own "stuff" under control, our opponents will find it easy to push our buttons. When a button gets pushed, self-control is of the utmost importance.

One of my buttons has always been people who insist that they bear no personal responsibility for their theological beliefs. My Internet enemy would always claim that he had no problem with gay people, but God did, so he had no choice but to hate gay people. What a ridiculous argument! He would not even consider that perhaps God did not have any problem with gay people (that came from interpretations of Scripture, and we know how he felt about such things). He would not consider that this was merely his opinion based on his community's belief about God and Scripture.

No argument, no matter how reasoned or careful, could sway him from his position that God hates homosexuality and so to be right with God, he must hate it too. It made me crazy. It still does. But I've found that the best way to handle such people is to take Xena's advice and disengage as quickly as possible. If you choose to stay engaged with someone who is so entrenched in his or her beliefs, you may want to look for common ground on which you can agree with your attacker. However, given my experience with unreasonable attackers, it is best to cut your losses. Nothing you do or say can change their minds, and ironically, the more you argue with them, the more hardened their positions become. The possibility of ceding any common ground to someone with whom they so strongly disagree is threatening to them and stands a good chance of escalating the confrontation.

This is what happened to me on the Internet message board. The more I tried to find common ground with my opponent, the more belligerent and entrenched in his truth he became. It became a vicious circle. Instead of continuing, I bid him God's blessings and stopped exchanging messages with him. With no one to argue against, he eventually let the matter drop and moved on to other topics. When we exercise the self-control required to simply stop arguing with someone like this, we have mastered the art of the gentle reply. We have learned to be happy instead of needing to have someone else affirm that we are right.

In the heat of the moment, our answers (even if they are answers cutting off further communication) must always be gentle and reverent, respectful of the opponent. Later, when the battle is over, we can look for ways to deactivate the button that was pushed in us so that we're not emotionally rocked the next time this argument arises.

We deactivate those buttons by spending time in prayer and meditation after any attack that leaves us frustrated or doubting our own faith. After the most frustrating encounters with my Internet antagonist, I had to admit that I had no answers to satisfy him. Nothing I could say could deter him from his beliefs or his line of thinking. Instead of continuing to focus on him and the frustration he caused me, I had to go back to myself and figure out why his views got me so irritated. I realized it was my own control issues that were getting in the way. I believed that if I made a sound, reasoned argument, he would see the error of his ways and recant. I believed I could single-handedly change this man's mind. I realized that he and I both wanted the same thing—to be proved right, to have our views validated by someone who disagreed with them at first. We wanted to save one another from our perceived misconceptions.

That led me to begin thinking about other areas of my life where I've tried to save or control others with whom I disagreed. I would argue my points forcefully when I thought others were wrong about trivial things like which route is best to take to a certain destination or who sang some particular song. I wanted to be right. I wanted to save others from the embarrassment of making a mistake. My Internet antagonist told me the same thing. He wanted to save me from my mistaken theology. He wanted to save me from a "perverted homosexual lifestyle" that would surely lead me to hell. He wanted the satisfaction of being right—and so did I. When I gave up my need to be right—not just with my Internet antagonist, but with other disagreements in my life—and focused instead on being happy, that button no longer worked.

Treat Enemies with Respect

The Golden Rule will always apply when we deal with those who oppose us. We must treat them as we wish to be treated. If we want our enemies to respect us, we must treat them respectfully, but we should never let them off the hook. We still need to challenge them. This is where Bagger's advice to treat our opponent "without mercy" comes in. Often we are too nice to our opponents, letting them take advantage of us. Treating them "without mercy" means that we don't allow them to go away unchallenged.

There is a difference between Steven Pressfield's use of the word *mercy* and the Bible's. When the word *mercy* appears in the Bible, it means "compassion for the misery of others." The goal of mercy, in the biblical sense, then, would be to share in the suffering of others. For Pressfield, however, "having mercy" for an opponent means simply letting them spout their ill-informed opinions without challenge. We allow them to remain in their ignorance. If we are to contend with our enemies then, we must do so "without mercy"—without sympathizing with them and without letting them off the hook.

Jesus understood the difference. He knew what it meant to treat his opponents with infinite respect but without mercy. Jesus regularly faced critics in the form of Pharisees and other religious and political leaders of his day. He was not afraid to contend with them. He often called them "vipers" and "hypocrites." He even went into one of their houses of worship and upended the tables. He never lost respect for his opponents, but he always contended with them "without mercy," and he was never afraid to contend to the death.

We can follow Jesus' example when we deal with our own enemies. Jesus never allowed the Scribes and Pharisees to define him—though they tried, deriding him for associating with tax collectors and sinners (Mark 2:16). When challenged, he often turned the arguments used against him on their heads, refusing to accept his opponents' framing of the moral issues of his day. He openly flaunted religious edicts by reaping and healing on the Sabbath (Mark 2:23ff., 3:1ff.), among other outrageous acts.

We, too, must not allow our opponents to define us or accept their framing of the morality of our lives. Our opponents so often come with the preconceived notion that we are "living in sin" by simply being who God created us to be that we may always feel on the defensive. We must take a page from Jesus' playbook and begin to turn the tables on those who begin with the assumption that simply being a gay, lesbian, bisexual, or transgender person equals a sinful life. Refuse to start from their premise. Reframe the argument.

On the *Whosoever* e-mail chat list, a member asked the group how we would explain that homosexuality is a moral good. She noted that when we are asked this question, we "change the subject" instead of arguing for the moral goodness of homosexuality. The main reply to the question was, "Why is it necessary to explain homosexuality as a moral good?" No one ever asks heterosexuals to justify their sexual orientation as a "moral good." It's like asking, "When did you stop beating your spouse?" The question makes assumptions not in evidence and immediately puts one on the defensive. Even worse, one cannot answer the question without implying that at least some of its assumptions are correct. Thus the question regarding the "moral goodness" of a person's orientation stems from the spurious belief that somehow the very existence of homosexuality is a "moral bad" in need of justification. But there is no moral goodness or badness to sexual orientation; it just is. That is why it is important to recognize that religious opposition to homosexuality is not the "other side" of the issue as the media present it. There are no sides in the matter.

When we are challenged with religious questions presented as the "other side" of the GLBT issue, we can follow Jesus' example and change the subject, redefining the issue away from the spurious religious spin. Jesus constantly challenged those who sought to impose their own beliefs on him; he knew that their views were not the "other side" of the issues he came to address. When he healed the man with the withered hand on the Sabbath in Mark 3, the Pharisees were hoping that he would break Sabbath law so that they could conspire to have him arrested and executed. Jesus redefines the issue for them by asking, "Is it lawful to do good or to do harm on the Sabbath, to save life or to kill?" (Mark 3:4). The Pharisees may have made an exception to healing on the Sabbath if it saved a life, but they were not about to give Jesus an inch. They were determined to trap Jesus, and if he healed on the Sabbath, they had their evidence, especially since the man with the withered hand was in no danger of dying that day. Jesus treated the Pharisees with infinite respect but without mercy. Their hardness of heart and determination to expose Jesus as someone who was morally corrupt angered Jesus, and he healed the sick man despite the consequences.

We must act in the same way, not allowing our opponents to set the framework for the discussion, since they are not the "other side" of the issue. We must give them infinite respect but treat them without mercy. To do otherwise is to give their belief in our "sinfulness" a validity that it does not deserve. When an argument begins from a premise of inherent sinfulness, we must change the starting point from a question of morality to a question of love. The Bible tells us that where love is, God is, since God is love (1 John 4:7). When we have love, we have God. Gay, lesbian, bisexual, and transgender relationships that are based in love have God present in them. The "moral good" of homosexuality—or heterosexuality, for that matter—comes from that sexual orientation being rooted in love. If any sexual orientation has a "moral bad," it is a relationship not grounded in love—regardless of the orientation of the partners.

In addition, we must remember that God sees us not as genders but as beloved children. There is no male or female—we are all one in Christ Jesus according to Galatians 3:28. If this is true, God would not even take notice of homosexuals or transgender persons. What God looks for in us is love. Indeed, if Jesus is to be believed, all the laws and the prophets hang on the quality of our love for God, self, and neighbor (Matthew 22:37–40). If we have love, we have God. We are not our sex or our sexual orientation—we are our love. This is the starting point for all arguments about "morality" and "sinfulness"—a starting point that treats the opponent with infinite respect but without mercy.

I treated that young African American questioner at the town hall meeting with infinite respect but without mercy. I was not about to let him think that his point (and his preconceived notions about GLBT relationships) was valid. He was not speaking to the "other side" of the issue. I pointed out that when the Supreme Court struck down antimiscegenation laws in 1967 in *Loving* v. *Virginia*, polls showed that 73 percent of Americans still supported a ban on interracial marriage. My questioner was willing to leave *my* right to marry the one I love up to the majority opinion but not his own. That belief was something that needed to be challenged.

I would hope that my enemies would treat me the same way and challenge me when I hold erroneous beliefs. It is not a sign of weakness to change one's position when it is shown to be wrong. I am always grateful to those who correct me before I look foolish in front of a crowded auditorium—even if I consider that person my enemy.

We must be careful, however, when we treat opponents "without mercy" that it is never our intention to humiliate or dehumanize them. As GLBT Christians, we are used to being dehumanized, but we should never resort to that tactic ourselves. We know how harmful it is, and that alone is reason enough to never make another human being experience those harsh feelings. We must always remember, as Jesus certainly did, that our opponents are human beings—misguided, perhaps, but always human beings, made and loved by their Creator.

We must remember that the concern from some of those who oppose us may well be genuine. Our opponents truly believe that as GLBT people, we are not "saved" and will therefore be cast into hell for eternity. Some are so convinced of this view that they will speak harshly to us in an effort to literally "scare the hell" out of us. My brother-in-law's concern springs from this deeply held belief. He's afraid I'll go to hell, so he will contend with me to the death, if necessary, to save my soul. We must understand that our opponents often see themselves as genuine heroes of the story—the ones who are appointed to keep us from an eternity of torture. They take their job seriously, and their attacks on us often come from a place of genuine concern. We need to be clear that we understand and appreciate their concern, but we are secure in our salvation. Show their view infinite respect, but do not give this view any mercy. We, as GLBT Christians, are bound not for damnation but for salvation. We have God's grace just as surely as our opponents do. Never forget that. If an opponent becomes too insistent, watch for the warning signs of becoming entangled in a pointless argument, and follow Xena's advice: run.

Deeper conversation with our opponents is possible when we understand their motivations and we can put aside our need to be right and instead seek relationship. Two friends of mine, Dotti Berry and Roby Sapp, are prime examples of people who show infinite respect to their opponents but no mercy. They began having regular lunches with a man named "Pastor Jay," whom they met during a panel discussion on same-sex marriage in 2004. Pastor Jay was at the time with a congregation in Bellingham, Washington.

Dotti wrote on the couple's Web site (http://www. gayintostraightamerica.com) about their experience with Pastor Jay: "After about six months, Pastor Jay said, 'I can't deny the love I see between the two of you, and that has changed me.' Pastor Jay says he now supports holy unions and civil unions for us, but has continued to say he isn't quite there on 'marriage.' He admitted at [a recent] lunch, however, that he is now asking himself, 'Why not marriage?' [Our lunches have] caused him to look more deeply at the meaning of marriage, asking, 'What does marriage mean?'"[4]

This is what can happen when we treat our opponents with infinite respect and without mercy. Dotti and Roby simply took the time to get to know Pastor Jay and to let him get to know them. They challenged his assumptions and would not let him abdicate responsibility for his beliefs. They contended with him to the death—an enemy died, and in his place, an ally was born. They are the embodiment of bulletproof faith in action.

See God in Our Opponents

Dotti and Roby could treat Pastor Jay with the infinite respect he deserved because they understood that the same God that dwelled within them dwelled in Pastor Jay as well. It was difficult for me to see God in my Internet antagonist. He refused to be vulnerable with me. He never trusted me. He never opened up to me because he feared that I would use his vulnerabilities against him (as he had done to me).

It wasn't until I realized how valuable he had been to me that I saw the holiness in this man. I consider my Internet antagonist a friend of mine because he made me a better person—one who is prepared to pass on that gift and help others in their faith journey. It's not exactly what he intended when we began swapping posts. He intended to change my mind. He intended to warn me about the fires of hell that awaited me if I didn't repent of my sexual orientation. But God had a different intent for our relationship and used it to strengthen my faith and renew my spirit. I posted a message thanking my Internet friend for all he had done for me. I never received a reply, but I am grateful for him and the divinity that lives within him. We may never agree on anything, but I know that God is alive and well in him and that the amazing grace of God will lead him.

It's difficult for GLBT people to see any trace of God in the people who persecute us most zealously. Seeing God in anyone who condemns or works against the best interest of GLBT people can be a challenge. Remember, though, that we are not required to like our enemies, but we must love them. We must strive to see the holy even in the most profane. We must make an effort every day to see the glory of God in each person, even if it is hiding under a bushel of bigotry.

God may shine dimly in the lives of those who persecute us, but rest assured, God is there. Our job is not to change those who oppose us but to change ourselves—to become bulletproof—and recognize that even those who speak the most vitriol against us are as imbued with God as we are.

Do Not Fear Contradictions

When I hear opponents of homosexuality speak so confidently about their conviction that God condemns us, it can give me pause. Having a bulletproof faith doesn't mean that the old tapes telling us we're sick and sinful don't get played from time to time. It does mean that we don't give in to those old messages of self-hatred. Instead, we understand that while our view may conflict with those who oppose us, it doesn't mean that our faith is wrong.

It's hard, however, to hear repeated attacks against GLBT Christians without pausing to wonder if they are right and we are wrong. That's a natural reaction. Especially since the majority of us come from religious backgrounds that taught us from the cradle that traditional theology confirms that God loathes homosexuals. My brother-in-law underscored this point for me during our argument. He insisted that since our positions are so contradictory, one of us *must* be wrong. We cannot both be right.

It is this kind of logic that keeps many GLBT Christians trapped in the closet, afraid to step forward in spirit and in truth. Their experience of God has flatly contradicted the teachings of their church, but they believe that since their opponents' argument was there first—or is claimed as "tradition"—it must be right. Sadly, they will deny their experience of God and repress their authentic selves, all in the name of "tradition."

I tried to explain to my brother-in-law that contradictions are nothing to fear. The Bible tells us we see things on this side of eternity through a glass darkly. Not one of us sees the entire picture. We only have pieces of truth here on earth. It's like putting together a giant jigsaw puzzle. Two pieces, even from the same puzzle, when laid side by side, can appear to be contradictory. They can appear to not be part of the same puzzle, but when we put those pieces together—when we dialogue with other Christians, with people of other faiths, and with those who shun faith altogether—we begin to get an inkling of what the bigger picture must look like. We begin to understand that every single person in this world is part of God's puzzle and has an important part to play in the bigger picture.

God is the only one working from the picture on the box top. We, as pieces of truth, are constantly searching for those other truths that fit what we know to be true. We find ourselves in communities of like-minded believers, and we find a fit. The incredible thing—the miraculous thing—is when we find ourselves with people who disagree with us but we still discover God's truth. Dotti and Roby found that with Pastor Jay, and even more important, Pastor Jay found that with Dotti and Roby. They reached across the divide and found a kindred spirit there. It's that final piece of the puzzle that joins the land and sky, the mountain and the river and makes the picture complete.

There are no unimportant pieces to God's puzzle. There are no rejected pieces of the puzzle. There are no contradictory pieces to the puzzle. We all fit into God's plan somehow. Faith is the necessary ingredient we little puzzle pieces need. We need to know, without a doubt, that despite the contradictory beliefs held by those who oppose us, they are pieces of God's puzzle just as surely as we are. We become bulletproof when those contradictions do not shake us but instead move us to seek common ground with our opponents—places where our truths fit together. It is grace that allows us to continue to love one another despite all differences. It is grace that allows us to move forward together toward God in full knowledge that we don't have to have all the answers; all we need is love, hope, and faith.

That's not to say that all contradictory positions are fine. We do have to judge whether someone's belief could truly come from the God we know and experience. I remember watching a documentary about antiabortion activists where one burly, bearded man looked right into the camera and said that God had told him to shoot abortion doctors. It was chilling. The God of my experience would never order anyone to kill another human being. There are many ways to reconcile differences, and killing should never be among them.

Fred Phelps and his family routinely picket gay and lesbian events as well as funerals for soldiers killed in Iraq and Afghanistan. They say God has told them to hate fellow human beings simply because of whom those people love or the alleged actions of the country they served. The God of my experience would never condone this. Hatred of a fellow child of God is something alien to the God of grace and mercy that I have experienced. These are contradictory beliefs that I believe are not from God and not part of the puzzle God is putting together to bring about God's reign.

James 3:17 tells us that we can easily identify what comes from God. We know God is present when the message is "peaceable, gentle, open to reason and full of mercy and good fruits." Those who advocate the murder of fellow human beings do not speak for God, no matter how noble their cause may seem to them or others. Those who use abusive, combative words are not speaking for God. Those who are not open to reason are not speaking for God. Those who are not full of mercy or producing good fruit of the spirit are not speaking for God. Those who condemn anyone, be they GLBT people or other minorities, are not speaking words from God. Instead, they are speaking words formulated from their own bigotry. They claim God's blessing on their bigotry, but their words betray their true agenda.

More often than not, those messages that contradict our experiences of God are full of hatred, condemnation, and bigotry. They are words not from God but from fearful humans. We have nothing to fear from these contradictions as long as our bulletproof faith is grounded in our experience of God.

Laugh at Yourself

During my training as a spiritual director, one of our instructors was fond of saying, "Be gentle with yourself." She said it so often during the two-year program that it became a joke within the group. If tensions arose or someone began to feel overwhelmed, we'd say together, "Be gentle with yourself." It always broke the tension and made us smile, but it is excellent advice to anyone seeking a bulletproof faith.

When we take ourselves too seriously, we can become wrapped up in needing to be right and easily fall into the trap of getting stuck in a religious argument that we ultimately cannot win. When we cannot laugh at ourselves, it's easy to get drawn into arguments and lose our ability to speak gently and reverently to our opponents. It's imperative that we be gentle with ourselves, or the bullets may find a weak spot in our faith.

My Internet antagonist had no idea how to be gentle with himself or anyone else. He was the most humorless human being I have ever met. He believed that laughing or enjoying himself was somehow sinful. In his mind, being a good Christian meant being at all times serious and joyless. There are many Christians, both conservative and liberal, who believe the same thing. Those who believe, however, that God created us because God thought we might enjoy living understand that laughter is something God created as well. God intends for us to enjoy this life, and many studies have shown the health benefits of a good laugh.

I often had to break away from the Internet message boards because of how dreary it would be going back and forth with such a joyless person. If I spent too much time on the message board, I found myself becoming just as morose as my opponent. I had to just stop and realize that I needed to be gentle with myself. We all need to take a break from time to time and just relax and enjoy life. Don't be afraid to laugh at your own foibles and shortcomings. They are part of you—and blessed by God.

Know That Experience Trumps All

I have noted before that theology is often seen as the "four-legged stool" of Scripture, tradition, reason, and experience (in that order of importance), but some strains of Christianity eject experience from the mix and sit on a "three-legged stool." We minimize or remove experience from the theological mix at our own peril. A theology based on just Scripture, tradition, and reason is a theology empty of the Holy Spirit, who brings the experience of God into our lives.

Those who discount experience often say that we are not to trust our feelings. It's true that often our feelings have led us astray. Feelings of lust can lead one to cheat on a spouse or partner. Feelings of hatred can lead one to lash out at people and cause hurt feelings or acts of violence. Even feelings of love can lead to obsession if a love goes unrequited or is rebuffed. Those who only follow their feelings and nothing else are always making trouble for themselves and others, so I'd have to agree that listening *only* to your feelings can lead to trouble.

However, I'm not suggesting that we simply follow our feelings or go with our heart and act rashly or without wisdom. There's much more to experience than what we feel about it. The word *experience* comes from the Latin *experientia*, which means "the act of trying"; thus experience is knowledge gained through repeated trials. It doesn't mean a feeling gained during repeated trials. It means *knowledge*. When we experience something over and over again, we don't simply feel it; we *know* it. Experience brings wisdom and the ability to sort through our feelings and identify what is emotionalism and what is knowledge gained through our experiences. We come to this knowledge by testing and trying. The Bible tells us that we are not simply to accept what comes to us as being from God but to "test the spirits" (1 John 4:1). Are they "peaceable, gentle, open to reason and full of mercy and good fruits"? When we test and try those things that come our way, we begin to understand and gain the knowledge needed to recognize God in any experience that we have.

Those who discount experience as an avenue to God forget that without experience, we would not have Scripture, tradition, or reason. It is through their experiences of God that the ancient writers were moved to jot down their thoughts about God in the first place. If they had never experienced God, they never would have put quill to parchment and written down anything worthwhile. Likewise, without repeated experiences, we would not have any traditions to pass down. Traditions come about because of repeated experiences that instill knowledge and wisdom. Without the Scripture and traditions that came through repeated experiences of God, we would not have the ability to use our reason to keep revising our notions of Scripture and tradition as our knowledge grows. Experience is the key. Everything we know about God comes to us through our experience of God. Tossing experience from the mix or labeling it as rash emotionalism is like cutting off our head. We cannot exist without our experience of God.

Since experience means testing and trying the events of life that come to us, our experiences can change us over time. We see this change in the pages of Scripture itself. In the Old Testament, the ancient Hebrews attributed everything to God, from wars to the mass slaughter of infants to direct orders to sacrifice a beloved child. The cultural experience of those Old Testament writers was one of war and harsh survival.

Reading through the Old Testament and then comparing it to the New Testament, we have to wonder if God has changed. The God that ordered wars and slaughters seems to change into a loving and merciful God who counsels us to strive for peace with everyone (Hebrews 12:14), avoid stupid controversies and arguments over the law (Titus 3:9), forgive one another and end bitterness and malice (Ephesians 4:31–32), and not repay evil for evil (1 Thessalonians 5:15). Even Jesus tells us that everything hangs on the commandment to love God, self, and neighbor. The New Testament is filled with love talk, telling us that love is of God (1 John 4:7) and that love trumps even faith, hope, and charity (1 Corinthians 13).

Did God change? No, God has always remained the same. We have changed as our experiences of God have deepened. The ancient Hebrews may have encountered God as warlike, but humanity's experience through Jesus revealed a previously unexamined side of God. Jesus brought us a new experience of God, a loving, grace-filled God. Through Jesus, we understand that our warring nature, our penchant for dividing the world into "us" and "them," is a product of our self-absorption and disconnection from God. God neither orders us to war against one another nor takes sides when we do take up arms. Instead, God calls us to turn from our warring ways. God calls us to stop focusing on our selfish and fearful view that anyone different from ourselves is an enemy to be defeated or destroyed.

Jesus calls us to put away our childish beliefs that God takes sides or orders us to harm other living beings. Jesus shows us that God expects us to work cooperatively to bring about God's kingdom. Any experience that teaches us to put up barriers between ourselves and others is not an experience from God. The ancient Hebrews had an inkling of this God. Even though they attributed vengeance and war to God, they still had laws showing mercy to strangers, widows, and the poor. Indeed, Jesus' greatest commandment to love comes directly from Old Testament law. The God of love was within the experience of the ancient Hebrews, but it wasn't until Jesus revealed the full nature of God that we came to understand that it is not God's will for us to divide and battle against one another. Many of us are still learning that lesson.

A good rule of thumb for figuring out whether your experiences in this life are ones that reveal God is found in the old cliché "You know you've created God in your own image when He hates the same people you do." When we attribute our dislike of others or our animosity toward others to God or our understanding of God, it is a clear signal that we are using God to justify our own prejudices. Those who believe that GLBT people are the greatest threat to society or the church and justify those beliefs by quoting the Bible or talking about God are projecting their own fears and bigotry onto God. One cannot hate anyone and attribute that attitude to God. That goes for us as well as it does for those who oppose us. 1 John 2:9 is clear that if we hate anyone, we cannot say that we have truly experienced God. The point is made again in 1 John 4:20: "Those who say, 'I love God,' and hate their brothers or sisters are liars; for those who do not love a brother or sister, whom they have seen, cannot love God, whom they have not seen."

It's simple, then: if any experience in our lives makes us more loving, more forgiving, more compassionate, more peaceful, or more accepting of others, we have certainly experienced the still living, still loving, still speaking God that Jesus came to reveal.

The Reality of Our Enemies

Though we are commanded to love our enemies and view them through the eyes of compassion and infinite respect, we should never doubt that our enemies are real and that their agenda is dedicated to our marginalization, if not our complete destruction. Mel White, in *Religion Gone Bad*, reveals the details of a secret summit held in 1994 at the Glen Eyrie conference center near Colorado Springs, Colorado. The fifty-five fundamentalist Christian leaders who attended came with just one goal: "to plan their 'short-term' solution for the problem of gay and lesbian Americans."[5]

It's important to understand that to the most extreme fundamentalists, our very lives are a "problem" in need of a "solution." Those who gathered at the meeting were dedicated to denying rights to GLBT people and curbing any political influence our community might have. Since that meeting, we've seen their agenda play out all over the country in the form of state constitutional amendments banning same-gender marriage, a federal form of the same amendment, and a push in some states to ban adoption by same-gender couples. Our lives were used as the main "wedge issue" in the presidential election in 2004, where so-called value voters went to the polls to vote against our right to marry and for candidates who promised to continue oppressing us. Fundamentalist Christian leaders have also thrown their support behind openly antigay candidates and still hold sway as a base voting bloc that many in the Republican Party are terrified to displease.

In an interview with *Whosoever* after the release of his book in 2006, White warned that we must take the Christian right seriously because its partisans seriously want to see us eliminated. Why do those on the Christian right believe that gay and lesbian people are such a threat to the nation? White said it has everything to do with what fundamentalist Christians call "God's chain of command."

"They see very clearly that the whole universe falls apart if order isn't kept," he said. "God created the order from God to Jesus, from Jesus to men, from men to their wives, from wives to their children. So men play a critical role in bridging the gap between the deity and the family. The human male is the person that God uses to bring the truth to the world and the family. If the man quits acting like a man and doesn't take the man's responsibilities—that's what they call gays—then the structure falls apart."[6]

There is also a deep sense within fundamentalist Christianity that God has bestowed special blessings on the United States of America—that we are indeed a chosen nation. They believe that granting full rights to GLBT people will anger God, according to White.

"So they've got to save the male role, but they also have to save the country for God's blessing. If the country recognizes us in any way like in hate crimes, domestic partnership, the military, or marriage—one of those official recognitions could be the final straw that will break God's back and have God pull away from us," he said.[7]

We've already experienced this argument when Jerry Falwell laid the blame for 9/11 at the feet of abortionists, feminists, gays and lesbians, the ACLU, and People for the American Way. The press blew it off as another odd rant from a Christian fundamentalist, but according to White, this is the heart of their belief. The perceived "lifestyles" of those on Jerry's list threatens God's chain of command. Women are out of their place, choosing when to reproduce, declaring independence from their men, and loving other women. Gay men have abandoned their role as real men and are no better than women, and heaven help the man whose gender identity is female. The misogyny of fundamentalist Christianity runs as deep as its homophobia. We ignore these fanatics at our own peril, White warned.

The God described by White is alien to me, and I'm thankful for that. I was raised in a Southern Baptist church that believed this philosophy to its core, but it never resonated with me. It never made any sense. If that was truly how God acted in the world, it was a God I never wanted to get to know. He (and believe me, this God is *always* a he) seemed petty, mean, and vicious. Oddly enough, so were the people who believed wholeheartedly in this God.

Christian fundamentalists suffer from a classic case of creating God in their own image. It's true that our enemies are using God to further their own prejudices, but this is precisely what makes them so dangerous to us. There is nothing they won't do to see that we are marginalized or crushed as a community, and they'll claim God's blessing for it every step of the way. We must be ready to contend with them, offering infinite respect but showing no mercy. Our faith must be bulletproof, or we will be tempted to hate them or give up our faith in despair because of their hateful tactics against us. We must never be tempted to belittle them but must instead applaud their political brilliance while we work to advance God's unconditional love for everyone.

Putting Away Our Guns

While it is true that the GLBT community faces real threats from a segment of fundamentalist Christianity, we should not believe the media hype that there is only the extreme right and extreme left when it comes to religion. There is a vast religious middle made up of believers who are not being represented in the media and are largely ignored or taken for granted by both the extreme right and the extreme left.

Many within this vast middle may still believe that it is wrong or sinful to be gay, lesbian, bisexual, or transgender, but we do a disservice to ourselves and them to brand these people as enemies. If we approach those in the middle with guns blazing, assuming we know what our opponents think or feel and prejudging them, or approach with the attitude that we are superior or they are less than worthy of respect for their beliefs, we will never be able to find common ground with them. We will never be able to reach them and tell them our stories.

On Easter morning in 2006, Eric Elnes, then the pastor of Scottsdale Congregational United Church of Christ in Scottsdale, Arizona, set out with a few other people on CrossWalk America, a 2,500-mile journey from Arizona to Washington, D.C. They went with the intention of spreading a more progressive view of Christianity, believing the media hype that there were only two kinds of Christians—extremely conservative or extremely liberal. They walked to put action to the progressive principles they believed in that had been outlined in Elnes's book *The Phoenix Affirmations*.[8] What they discovered surprised all of them.

They were welcomed in places where they never expected to be welcomed. In Hereford, Texas, for example, a small, fairly conservative congregation was the only church that would welcome them. Elnes writes in his book *Asphalt Jesus* that the pastor at Fellowship of Believers was clear that while he and his congregation didn't agree with all of the Phoenix Affirmations (especially Affirmation 5, which speaks in support of GLBT believers), they were glad to welcome them.[9]

And welcome them they did—with an extravagant barbecue and party. The members opened their homes to the walkers and allowed Elnes to speak at their church on Sunday. Elnes writes that while some were visibly uncomfortable as he spoke about homosexuality, many confided in him afterward that they have gay family members. Other congregation members complimented the walkers on their kindness and wondered why anyone would not welcome them.

Reverend Tracy Dunn-Noland, the pastor at Fellowship of Believers, told Elnes the church supported them "because you didn't come with your guns out. You came with the desire to just make some new friends. And that's how change in going to happen in this country."[10]

This is how we must always approach anyone who disagrees with us—with our guns safely tucked away. We must be out to make friends with those who believe we are "sinful" because making friends out of people who oppose us is the best way to eliminate enemies. Certainly there are those who will not engage in conversation with us and will insist on attacking us—that's when Xena's strategy comes in handy: we must get away from them as fast as possible, but we do it without malice. We try to leave them better than we found them—blessed by our presence, even if they never feel it or acknowledge it.

After the long walk from Phoenix to Washington, Elnes is hopeful for the state of Christianity in America. He believes that the media are missing the story about our faith by focusing on the extremes. He and the other walkers did encounter conservative churches that would not welcome them, but they found common ground with more people than they expected. The religious leaders who are given attention by the media don't speak for them, and many feel they are without a voice. In fact, the words Elnes uses to describe those who are in the middle of the extremes of Christianity sound very much like what GLBT people have always felt: "Many Christians who yearn for a more inclusive, compassionate, and intellectually honest form of faith feel so alone, like they're the only ones who feel the way they do, but they're not. Even in the smallest towns in the most conservative areas, many people are not only sympathetic to these same desires but also actively gathering in house fellowships, book groups, and unsung churches around the country—or are yearning mightily to do so."[11]

Feeling as if they are the only ones feeling this way is an emotion with which we GLBT people can identify. If we can begin to feel compassion for those in the religious middle who feel left behind or misrepresented by the religious leaders who claim to speak for them, we can recognize the common ground we share. We, too, have known the sting of feeling abandoned, lost, or excluded. Though we may disagree on the subject of homosexuality—if we seek to simply understand one another and can trust God to work out the rest—we'll find many that we would have written off as enemies can become some of our staunchest allies. That is a gift we can gladly accept.

Spiritual Survival Tips

1. Refuse to receive the gift of insults from your enemies, but be grateful for the unintended gifts the enemies bring as they help you identify "hot button" issues still in need of healing within yourself.

2. Instead of fearing your enemies, recognize them as opportunities to learn more about their worldview and more about

yourself and how you react when confronted by someone who believes differently than you do.

3. Be grateful for what your enemies can teach you about yourself and your own faith. Use them as teachers to strengthen and deepen your own faith.

4. Learn self-control from enemies. Even if they make you feel angry or frustrated, refuse to be drawn into an angry exchange or to use harmful words with them. When the confrontation is over, work to deactivate the button in you that they pushed with their words or actions.

5. Always treat enemies with infinite respect, but do not allow them to walk all over you. Contending with them without mercy means that we cannot let unfounded or ill-conceived opinions go unchallenged. Our manner, however, must be gentle and loving.

6. We must learn to see God in our enemies, no matter how difficult or harmful their words or deeds may be. We must remember that no matter how misguided or angry they are, they are still God's beloved children. Even in the face of abuse, always respond with gentleness.

7. Don't give in to any message, internal or external, that says you are sick or sinful for being gay, lesbian, bisexual, or transgender. Our belief that God loves us and accepts us as God made us may contradict the beliefs of people who oppose us, but God's plan includes us all, despite any seeming contradictions.

8. Be gentle with yourself. Take frequent breaks from confrontations or dialogues with those who oppose us. Be sure to spend time with loving, supportive friends and communities to recharge your batteries and reconnect with God.

9. Trust your own experience of God over what other people say, no matter what authority they claim. We can easily identify God experiences because they lead us to become more gentle, peaceable, and reasonable.

10. Never forget that our enemies are real. They may claim that GLBT people have an agenda, but we certainly know that they do. Our enemies are working to strip us of our civil rights and keep us from being fully accepted in the church.

11. Reach out to those in the religious middle. There are many religious people who do not identify with fundamentalist Christianity. We need to be willing to begin a dialogue that can transform them from enemies into allies.

SPIRITUAL SURVIVAL EXERCISE:
BREATHING INTO OUR PAIN

It felt like a hot knife cutting into my shoulder blade. It was an exquisite pain; I wasn't sure whether to clench my teeth and bear it or scream and fight back.

It wasn't a knife in my back, however. It was the fingertip of my massage therapist. The pressure against the muscles of my shoulder blade produced a sharp, stinging pain, and my mind reacted on automatic—but it was a familiar pain, one I had experienced many times before. Though the pain was excruciating, both my mind and my body understood it to be good pain, because after the pain, the tense muscle would relax and begin to heal. After a few minutes of pain, relief would come, and the result would be a pain-free shoulder blade.

That knowledge didn't keep the pain from taking my breath away the moment I first felt it. I had to make myself consciously relax into the pain. I had to concentrate on the source of the pain and give the muscles permission to release the tension of the day and begin their healing process.

Attacks on our faith are sometimes breathtaking in the same way. They leave us feeling weak and throbbing with mental and spiritual pain. They cut our emotions like a knife and often hurt physically, twisting our stomach into knots, leaving us sickened and short of breath. In these moments, we need to practice breathing into our pain. We need to practice giving our mental, spiritual, and physical muscles the permission to relax, even amid the pain and anguish caused by the onslaught of condemning words.

The time to practice breathing into our pain is now, before we find ourselves faced with a loud protester or a family member using the Bible to condemn us. We've all faced these kinds of painful attacks, even if they have been indirect in the form of an antigay article in the newspaper or an antigay sermon from a television or radio preacher.

To begin this exercise, find a quiet place where you won't be disturbed and can devote fifteen to twenty minutes to this practice. Sit comfortably in a chair or on a mat on the floor—wherever you can be comfortable and alert without going to sleep. Close your eyes, and spend the first few minutes breathing in and out, paying attention to your breath. Do not try to change your breathing; simply observe it. Is your breathing shallow? Are you breathing deeply or erratically? Where is your breath coming from—your chest, your belly, your stomach? Feel the warmth of your breath in your nostrils as you exhale and the cool sensation as you inhale. Feel your lungs fill and expand as you inhale and empty as you exhale. Be keenly aware of any sensations in your body—aches, pains, itches, tingles. Simply experience the feeling of being in your body. Follow your breath as best you can until your mind begins to calm and your muscles start to relax.

As you enter a state of relaxation, call to mind an incident or situation in which you felt threatened or condemned as a gay, lesbian, bisexual, or transgender person. It could be a protester yelling condemnation, a preacher telling you God hates you, a family member expressing worry about your eternal soul, a friend shunning you because of your "lifestyle choice," or an antigay sermon or story you heard on the television or radio or read in a magazine or newspaper. Recall the words used in the attack— repeat them to yourself: "God hates fags!" "Turn or burn!" "Gays are an abomination!" "Gay people are condemned to hell!" "Gay people are no better than animals!" "Transgender people are an abomination!" Hear the vitriol in the words. Imagine the faces of the people saying them. See the anger in their faces.

See the disgust in their faces. Hear the hatred in their voices. Feel the sharp edges of the words they use.

How does this make you feel? Do you feel weak? What are the sensations in your body? Where is the pain—your stomach, your head, your shoulders, your chest? Does it feel like a knife, a punch, a kick? Check back with your breath—are you breathing heavier, faster? Is your heart beating faster? Are you palms getting wet? Are you feeling anxious and upset?

Now, imagine that this is exactly how your attacker feels.

The nature of an attack is that both the attacker and the attacked are in a heightened state of anxiety. The attacker is pumped up, on the offensive, ready to do battle. The one under attack is reacting defensively, ready for fight or flight. Nothing good comes from two people being in this state—nothing but pain and destruction will ensue. The cycle will never be broken unless one party remains calm and collected. The attacker is already agitated and spoiling for a fight. As those on the receiving end of the attack, it is our duty to break the cycle—to be the one who calmly deflects any attack—without anxiousness or anger.

As you imagine the assault continuing, begin to tune out the attacker's words. You've heard them all before; they have no power beyond the emotional impact and control over you that you give them. Deny the words permission to enter your mind, your heart, and your soul. Use your shield of faith to deflect the bullets of condemnation. Let the words melt into incomprehensible sounds.

Instead, focus your attention on the face and gestures of your attacker. Look closely—the face is contorting in anger as the insults spew from the mouth. Look deeply into the person's eyes—ask yourself what kind of pain that person has encountered in life. Open your heart to the person attacking you. Feel nothing but compassion for the pain and anguish that brought the person to this place. Ask yourself what it is that has hurt your attacker so deeply that he or she feels the need to lash out at you? If it is a family member or someone you know, perhaps you have some knowledge about the past and how the person may have been abused or hurt by religion or instilled with some deep fear of being abandoned or unloved by God. Reflect on this knowledge, and share the person's fear and anger.

When the anxiety of being attacked begins to affect you physically, mentally, and spiritually, the first thing you want to do is stop those feelings. You want to feel better. This is exactly what you should want for your attacker as well. If we are to love our neighbor as ourselves, we should not seek to end just our own suffering but the other's suffering as well.

As you imagine the attack continuing, begin to breathe into your own pain. Feel deeply the anger, the hurt, the despair, the sense of helplessness and worthlessness that the attack produces in you. Know that these are exactly the feelings your attacker is experiencing. Feel your heart breaking for your attacker. Recognize that he or she is a human being who wants the same things you want—peace, security, a sense of self-worth, a connection with God, and a feeling of being OK with God. Instead, like you, the other person may be feeling angry, hurt, in despair, helpless, and worthless. A belief that this person holds dear, for good or ill, is under attack by your mere existence. You, personally, have nothing to do with those feelings, but simply by being who you are, you've touched a nerve that triggers the need to lash out at you to salve your attacker's own fear and anger.

How would you want someone to treat you when you're feeling angry, hurt, in despair, helpless, and worthless? Would you want someone yelling at you, berating you, and condemning you? Certainly not! Refuse to return hatred for hatred. Instead, use the power of love to overcome the violent words aimed at you. Imagine yourself standing silently, breathing deeply, and smiling at your attacker. Soften your heart toward the person, and send thoughts of love, thoughts of hope, thoughts of joy and peace. Send thoughts of innate worth. Tell the person that he or she is God's beloved child.

Should the assault continue, refuse to be drawn into the emotional anguish. Concentrate on your breath—breathe deeply and slowly. Breathe into your own pain. Concentrate on your heart rate—deliberately try to slow it down. Concentrate on your body—relax your tense, defensive muscles. Remain open and compassionate, even as the assault continues.

I've done this practice before with antigay protesters. Often it infuriates them even more because you are not reacting as they expect. Remember, the protester at my church flew into a rage when I simply said, "God bless you." People who mount these attacks are trying to goad you into a fight—a war of words. It helps them justify their own feelings of spiritual supremacy. Arguing with them validates them, and no matter how the argument goes, they will always feel that they have won—mainly because they drew you in, and now they can tell everyone that GLBT people have been mean and abusive to *them!*

Do not give in. As you continue your practice, imagine your attacker growing even more agitated and you growing calmer and calmer. Intensify your feelings of sending love and compassion to your attacker. Repeat the phrase "May you feel loving-kindness, may you feel God's peace." Send feelings of love and peace with all your heart. Send the feelings you most want for yourself. Love your opponent just as much as you love yourself.

Now imagine that you are turning from your attacker and walking away. The voice grows fainter in the distance. Your body relaxes, your breathing returns to normal, your heart slows as you return to a calm and relaxed state. The pain of the event begins to ease. Keep the attacker in mind, and send one more affirmation of God's love. Send yourself the same affirmation: "God loves you. God loves me. God's love is the same for all."

Take a few minutes to come back into your body. Thank God for being with you during the experience; then open your eyes. Just as a few moments of pain in your muscle can help your muscle better cope with future pain, so can experiencing the pain of this exercise help you cope better with the pain of a real-life attack. Breathe into your pain now, before the attacks come. Train your mind, body, and soul how to react to this pain, and when attacks do come, you'll find yourself calm and ready with a gentle and reverent response.

7

THE ONLY THING THAT COUNTS

> . . . The only thing that counts is faith working through love.
>
> —*Galatians 5:6*

To this point, we've talked a lot about faith and what makes it bulletproof. What exactly do we mean when we use the word *faith*? Hebrews 11:1 defines faith as "the assurance of things hoped for, the conviction of things not seen." The essence of a bulletproof faith is this assurance, this conviction—this deep knowledge, grounded in experience—that everything will be all right. No matter the challenges we face or the foes we do battle with, we have a home when we have that faith.

Dictionaries define *faith* as "belief or confidence in someone or something," but that belief can be in things that lack logical or concrete proof. This is the conviction of things not seen. Not one of us has seen God—not in any sort of human, concrete, or logically provable form—yet we have faith that God is real, present, and working in and through our lives. We have that assurance because even though we have not seen God, we have had concrete experiences of God in our lives. Coincidences, odd occurrences, happy accidents, and downright honest-to-God miracles have touched each of our lives in various ways, making God's presence real to us. Sometimes these are more real than if God had physically stepped out of the shadows and said, "Hi, there!"

Putting our faith in real things like cars, world leaders, and even organizations created to do good work in the world will lead only to disappointment. All these things can fail—and have done so in the past. However, when we place our faith in

God—when we believe in things that we hope for, things that we have yet to see—we are richly rewarded. We know that no matter where we go in the world, God will be there for us. Faith placed on our inward experiences—our inward knowledge—of God is the only faith that endures. It is the only faith that does not fail us in any ultimate way.

You're Not the Lone Ranger

When we gay, lesbian, bisexual, and transgender individuals despair over our faith or our place within the larger Christian community, we need to remember that we are not the first—and I fear, not the last—group of people to be marginalized and excluded by the church. We are merely the latest group of people to have their faith questioned, challenged, denied, and excluded from the larger body of Christ. Since Jesus' death and resurrection, members of our common faith have been fighting to deny grace to other groups who do not fit their "orthodox" idea of what constitutes a "true" Christian.

The Gentiles were the first group to be shunned by good, orthodox Christians. *Gentile* was the term used for anyone outside the Jewish religion and was usually used in a pejorative or derogatory way, in much the same way *fag* or *dyke* is used to demean gay and lesbian people today. In the years after Jesus' execution, Jewish Christians rejected the idea that Gentiles could be part of God's realm. We see that beginning to change in the book of Acts.

Acts 8:26–40 recounts the story of the apostle Philip, who meets a Gentile, a eunuch from Ethiopia, traveling from Jerusalem to Gaza. The eunuch was reading the Hebrew scriptures but was having trouble understanding them. Philip joins him in his chariot and teaches him about Jesus. As they come to a body of water, the eunuch asks, "What is to prevent me from being baptized?" Philip couldn't think of one thing, so he baptizes the eunuch.

It's important to understand the role of eunuchs in ancient society. They were often charged with serving in the bedchambers of women. Many of them had been castrated, but others were apparently genitally intact but had no interest in sex with women, so they were deemed "safe" to be around women. There are some scholars, like Toby Johnson, who believe that eunuchs were actually gay men, so they certainly could be trusted around a wife or other women in the family or community.[1] Church tradition teaches that the eunuch baptized by Philip went on to become the first Christian missionary to Africa. Given the anti-GLBT Christian traditions arising in Africa today, especially among the Anglican Church, it's ironic that they might never have heard the gospel were it not for a gay Gentile!

In Acts 11, God's acceptance of the Gentiles is reaffirmed when Peter reported having an odd vision involving a great sheet that descended from heaven. On the sheet were animals that had been declared "unclean" and therefore were forbidden to be eaten by observant Jews. However, Peter heard the Lord command him to "Rise. Kill and eat" (Acts 11:7). When Peter refused, he heard God say, "What God has made clean, you must not call profane" (Acts 11:9b).

Peter could have interpreted this dream in many ways, but he took it as a sign that God had accepted not just Jews but Gentiles as well. He visited Cornelius, a Gentile who is described as "a centurion, an upright and God-fearing man" (Acts 10:22). Peter's revelation continued as he met with Cornelius. He declared that "I truly understand that God shows no partiality" (Acts 10:34) and that "everyone who believes in [Jesus] receives forgiveness of sins through his name" (Acts 10:43). This is certainly very close to Jesus' own words in John 3:16 that "whosoever believes" is saved. Peter finally understands that no human distinction—be it of nationality, gender, race, or dare I add, sexual orientation or gender identity—is an ultimate barrier to God. God shows no partiality to any human being but accepts and loves them all.

Don't think that this was good news to those who were working with Peter. As soon as they heard about it, they criticized him and argued with him. Acts reports that the controversy ended quickly after he explained his vision, and the Holy Spirit fell upon the people present and gave them instant understanding (Acts 11:15).

Those most intimately involved with Peter may have quickly accepted the idea that Gentiles were also covered under God's grace and love, but the message took a while to get to those in outlying areas around the Holy Land. In Acts 15, Peter again defends his belief that Gentiles are included in God's realm at a meeting of the apostles and elders in Jerusalem. Some Jewish Christians were questioning this new teaching, and Peter reiterated that God made no distinction between Jewish and Gentile Christians. There is no report, however, that the Spirit descended on these Jewish Christians to convince them of the argument. There is evidence that these struggles continued, however, and Paul reported many controversies springing up between the Gentiles and Jewish Christians. In each instance, he soundly rebuked them for their rejection of the Gentiles.

In Romans 10:11–12, Paul reminded Jewish Christians that no one who believes will be put to shame. Why? Because just as Peter had said, God makes no distinction between people. God bestows riches on "all who call upon God." There is no exception in Paul's words—*all* who call upon God and believe are included in God's grace and mercy. No exceptions. No exclusions. No matter how much we want to exclude them. *All* believers are included in God's realm. Paul is clear that God has not called just the Jews to love God with all their heart, mind, and strength; God has called even those vile, sinful Gentiles. Paul sharply reminded the Jews that they must honor the call the Gentiles have received because "the gifts and the call of God are irrevocable" (Romans 11:29). Those gifts, that call, are for everyone who believes, be they gay, lesbian, bisexual, transgender, or straight. No one has the right to say that another person is not called for any reason.

In Romans 14, Paul addresses the controversy around the different eating habits of Gentiles and Jews. Some were insisting that strict Jewish eating guidelines should be observed, while others believed that they could eat anything because Christ had liberated them from the law. This echoes the argument over "behavior" that GLBT Christians often face. We are told that according to "God's law," sexual behavior should only be expressed between a husband and a wife, not between women and women or men and men. But if we truly believe that we have been liberated from the law through Christ, we understand that we are free to ignore the old law and celebrate our freedom. This is certainly not a freedom to sin—to use our sexual behavior in ways that abuse, use, or break covenant with another person. Our sexual behavior should always be expressed in loving, committed relationships, because God is present only where there is love. However, Paul's message is clear that we are not to judge one another for our behavior: "Those who eat must not despise those who abstain, and those who abstain must not pass judgment on those who eat; for God has welcomed them. Who are you to pass judgment on servants of another? It is before their own lord that they stand or fall. And they will be upheld, for the Lord is able to make them stand" (Romans 14:3–4).

Instead of judging one another for how we behave or what we eat, Paul advised that we "pursue what makes for peace and for mutual upbuilding" (Romans 14:19). Instead of judging one another on what we approve or disapprove of in each other, we need to put aside disagreements. We should stop putting stumbling blocks out over "behaviors" and "lifestyles" and get on with working together to realize God's realm. Paul calls on Jewish and Gentile Christians alike to put aside differences and work together.

Some people may object to comparisons between eating customs and sexual orientation, but laws around eating were taken seriously by Jewish Christians. Violation of these laws, in their opinion, would bar entrance to God's realm. Eating codes were just as important to Jewish Christians as sexual orientation is to modern-day fundamentalist Christians. For them, any violation of sexual codes that they subscribe to would be enough to bar someone from God's realm. Paul's answer, then, is a tough one for them (and for us) to follow. Paul says we need to stop judging one another for what each group approves and find common ground on which we can work together to accomplish God's plan for our world—a plan of unity, one body in Christ, concerned solely with reaching out and healing our broken world.

Eating was not the only area of controversy between Jewish and Gentile Christians. One of the biggest concerns was whether or not Gentiles seeking entrance into the Christian community should give up something that they were born with—an intimate part of themselves, their foreskins. This was the issue that Jewish Christians in Galatia faced. Some insisted that to be true followers of Jesus, the Galatians must submit to circumcision and follow Jewish law to the letter. In particular, these Jewish Christian teachers urged the men to submit to circumcision to prove their faith in Christ. If they refused, they were not true Christians. How many times do we, as GLBT Christians, get preached to about the "rules" we must follow or the things we must do to be considered Christian? I get letters almost daily telling me that I must believe this or that doctrine or that I must renounce my sexual orientation or else I am not a child of God or a true Christian.

Often, like the Galatian Gentiles, we are asked to prove our faith in an outward way by "circumcising" an innate part of our being—our sexuality. Only if we desire to become heterosexual can we truly be saved. Only if we observe the laws of "normal" society will we earn our right to be called "Christian" by society and the church at large. Until then, we are merely sinners pretending to have the grace of God.

Paul tells us to "stand firm" and not to "submit" to this "yoke of slavery" that often well-meaning Christians seek to put on us. By demanding that we first become heterosexual before we can be Christians, our detractors seek to put us into a form of slavery that forces us to deny our innate identity and live under a burden, a yoke of lies. In this way, we must cut off, or circumcise, our natural, God-given sexuality.

Paul warns us that if we let ourselves be circumcised, Christ will be of no benefit to us! If we renounce our God-given sexuality or gender identity, we will be trying to live by the law of today's church, which tells us that only heterosexuals are saved, and not by faith, which assures us that all who believe in Christ are saved. If we try to live by the law, Paul warns us, we cut ourselves off from Christ and fall away from grace. But the good news is that "In Christ Jesus neither circumcision nor uncircumcision counts for anything; the only thing that counts is faith working through love" (Galatians 5:6).

Read that last part very carefully. Just as Jesus told us that all the laws and the prophets hang on our love of God, neighbor, and self, Paul reiterates the command to love but adds faith— telling us that faith working *through* love is the *only* thing that counts. Sexual orientation or gender identity does not count. Like circumcision, making a change in something as inherent as our sexual orientation is worthless.

Indeed, faith is the common thread that runs through all the arguments from Philip to Peter to Paul. In all instances, what matters is the faith of the Gentile involved. The eunuch had faith. Cornelius had faith. Those with different eating habits and those who refused circumcision had faith. According to Paul, *faith working through love* is the only thing that counts. He told the Roman Jewish Christians who were concerned with eating practices, "Blessed are those who have no reason to condemn themselves because of what they approve . . . for whatever does not proceed from faith is sin" (Romans 14:22b–23).

If we act according to our faith in Christ—according to the love we have through our faith and trust in our experience of God in our lives—we commit no sin.

We might object, though, that those who work against us also claim to have faith, so isn't that the only thing that matters? The question leaves out the most important part of faith. It must be "working through love." Certainly those who work against the full inclusion of GLBT people in church and society say that they love us. We hear all the time about how much they love us but hate our "sin." Those who work for the exclusion of anyone in church and society may certainly have faith—but it is not a faith working through love.

Remember, 1 Corinthians 13 outlines the qualities of authentic love: patience, kindness, and the absence of envy, irritation, or resentment. Those who claim faith but hold signs and yell hateful words to anyone, be they GLBT people or families of military personnel attending funerals, are not working through love. Those who claim faith but arrogantly assert that God has told them GLBT people are inherently sinful or unworthy of civil rights or inclusion in the church are not working through love. Those who claim faith but insist that GLBT people must "circumcise" their sexual orientation before they will be found acceptable by God and the community are not working through love. Those who claim faith but are resentful that GLBT people are seeking equality in society and access to all levels of leadership within the church are not working through love. Those who rejoice at the continuing oppression of GLBT people in church and society and celebrate the victory of such measures as bans on same-gender marriage or the defeat of hate crimes or job equality legislation are not working through love.

Faith that is not working through love is based on things beyond the self. People whose faith is not working through love rely on religious councils, legislators, and their own power of persuasion (even if that means carrying signs with hateful words and being rude or mean) to advance their own ideas of God and faith in the world. Fundamentalist Christians have certainly made progress on their political and religious agendas as the entire nation fights over same-gender marriage and gay bishops. But this is not faith working through love. This is a faith based on human distortions of true Christian faith, and it is doomed to fail at some point.

Faith working through love has Jesus at its base, not the powers and institutions of the world. Following Jesus' lead, faith working through love seeks the inclusion of everyone. It seeks to spread the good news of God's love for everyone. When our faith is working through love, we are patient and kind. We are humble, not seeking our own way but seeking common ground where we can all grow as one in the body of Christ despite our differences. A faith working through love can work hard for equality within society and the church, but it does so by bringing people together on common issues of concern instead of building barriers and creating divisions.

The love on which this faith is founded will ultimately prevail in society and the church because the gentle voice of love and reconciliation is stronger than any loud voice of hatred or division. We must continue to put our faith in the Lord and not any earthly power because the ultimate power of love resides with God, and when we continue to practice that love on earth, it will surely manifest. We may not see the results of that gentle, powerful love come to fruition in our lifetime, but we must remember that God is stronger than any human institution. Same-gender marriage will one day be the law of the land despite mighty struggles against it because marriage is properly based on love, and love will win out. All discrimination against GLBT people will fall by the wayside because inclusion and fair treatment are the hallmarks of love, and love will always win.

Throughout history, oppression has always given way to inclusion. Don't be discouraged by political setbacks or the church's tortoise-paced movement toward inclusion. Our faith, working through love, will prevail. Work for equality and inclusion, but do it with gentleness and reverence, knowing that love will one day triumph over all human intolerance and hatred.

We must also resist the temptation to hate or dehumanize those who oppose us. Faith working through love does not rejoice when someone who believes differently is injured or cast out or discriminated against in any way. I was attending a continuing education class when my partner called to tell me that Reverend Jerry Falwell had died. My first reaction was deep sadness. Despite his past as a racist and a homophobe, this man had a family who loved him. He had children who would be missing a father, a wife who would be without her husband, and grandchildren who wouldn't get to sit on granddaddy's knee anymore. I grieved for Falwell, even though he worked tirelessly against our community in both the political and the religious arenas.

I expected a lot of rejoicing in the GLBT community over Falwell's death. I did see some of that, but to our community's merit, by and large we reacted kindly, extending our sympathy to Falwell's friends and family. While we disagreed with Falwell with every fiber of our being, the majority of our community remembered Falwell's humanity. This is what faith working through love looks like. It extends grace even to those with whom we disagree or who have done great harm to us personally or to the community to which we belong. This kind of bulletproof faith is the only thing that counts.

Spiritual Survival Tips

1. Do not put your faith in things or powers of the world—
   especially in the religious opinions of others. All these
   things will fail.

2. Never feel unworthy of God's love. Just as God declared
   the Gentiles "clean" and part of God's realm, God has also
   declared GLBT people to be God's beloved.

3. Do not let anyone tell you that you must change to be accepted by God. "Circumcising" your sexual orientation or gender identity is not required by God.

4. Make love your standard. Faith that does not work through love is not true faith.

5. Never belittle the faith of those who disagree with you or rejoice in their misfortune. Even those who oppose us have families and friends who love and care for them. We must cultivate that goodwill toward even our direst enemy.

8

YOU KNOW YOUR FAITH IS BULLETPROOF WHEN . . .

> Such faith takes for granted the tragedy of
> human life, the sin and stupidity of man and the
> catastrophic turmoil of nations. It is founded,
> not on the niceness of the world, but on inward
> awareness of adequate power to confront the world,
> despite devilish men and hellish circumstance.
> —*Harry Emerson Fosdick*, A Faith for Tough Times[1]

Even as we act confidently in our faith, we will almost certainly continue to experience doubt. With all the attacks GLBT people of faith face, doubt seems to be our constant companion. I imagine it was the constant companion of many of those early Gentiles who were also attacked and criticized for who they were. They had to become bulletproof in their faith to deal with the controversy that their lives created in the church. Doubt, however, is not something to be feared or avoided. In fact, one of the characteristics of a bulletproof faith is that it frequently encounters and embraces doubt. It is through our doubts that we are prompted to continue exploring our faith, growing our faith, testing our faith, and making our faith stronger. When we doubt, we seek relief. When we seek relief, we are forced to go deeper into our faith to find the answers we need to feel reassured in our faith.

As GLBT people of faith, we know doubt intimately. We have doubted our faith for so long that many of us may feel that doubt and faith are one and the same thing. Just when we think we've gotten our theological ducks in a row, some preacher or family member will shoot us down, call us "sinners," or insist we abandon our "sinful lifestyle" (whatever that is). We find ourselves plunged back into the depths of doubt. What if they are right and we are wrong? What if we really risk the fires of hell by believing that God loves us and made us just as we are and does not ask us to change or repent of our sexual orientation or gender identity?

The doubts can seem overwhelming at times—but we must remember, in the midst of our doubts, that we are not the only ones who have ever doubted our faith or felt abandoned by God. Even Mother Teresa, in *Come Be My Light,* a book published after her death, painfully revealed her own doubts and loss of faith. In one of her letters to Jesus she wrote, "In my heart there is no faith—no love—no trust—there is so much pain—the pain of longing, the pain of not being wanted. I want God with all the powers of my soul—and yet there between us—there is a terrible separation. . . . I do not doubt that it was You who called me, with so much love and force. It was You—I know. That is why the work is Yours and it is You even now—but I have no faith—I don't believe."[2]

Even Mother Teresa, a woman who worked tirelessly in service to others throughout her whole life, felt the sting of doubt, the pain of feeling abandoned by God. Yet she continued her work. She did not let her doubts, her fears, or her feelings of loneliness prevent her from working for God. She understood that if her feelings of separation from God brought others closer to God, then God's will was being worked through her life. If Mother Teresa can feel her own doubts, express them so painfully to Jesus, and yet not give up her struggle to help the least privileged among us, how could we even fathom letting a little doubt topple our faith?

We've all felt that separation from God, that feeling of not being wanted by God, but Mother Teresa teaches us to feel those feelings and then get on with serving God anyway. I believe that this kind of doubt is the greatest gift that God has given to GLBT people of faith. It is the constant challenge to our faith that makes our faith bulletproof. It is this deep doubt, knowing what total abandonment feels like, that ultimately keeps our faith strong—if we will let it.

The vast majority of Christians never have to think deeply about their faith or what it is based on. They are immediately accepted in any church they choose to wander into on any given Sunday. If they are heterosexual or from a respectable family or social class, our society ordinarily assumes them to be "good Christians." They easily accept the tenets of the faith, teach them to their Sunday school classes, listen to the preacher repeat them, and go about their lives believing them without question. They don't have to question any of these beliefs because nothing in their experience challenges those beliefs and everything outside of them affirms those beliefs.

The faith of GLBT people, by contrast, is constantly under assault. We are always questioning our beliefs and wondering whether we're being true to our experience of God or deluding ourselves. Our more conservative friends come down firmly on the side of delusion, but often their opinion is colored by their own unexamined faith. The presence of GLBT people of faith challenges their faith—a faith that isn't used to being challenged. Instead of questioning their own faith, they question *ours*. They insist that *their* faith must be right and *ours* must be wrong—but this isn't necessarily true. An unexamined faith is *not* a bulletproof faith. A faith based on a "this is what we've always believed" mentality is not a faith that can withstand doubt. Instead, that kind of faith must insist on its own way—by discounting or demeaning any faith that disagrees.

Remember, if our faith is doubted or questioned by others, it has nothing to do with us or our faith. That's "their stuff." Our faith has challenged them in a way that is unfamiliar to them. They've never had to question their faith. They've never had to examine what they believe and why. The preacher said it's in the Bible, and they believe it. That settles it for them. The appearance of a GLBT person of faith presents a danger to their own faith, so they lash out at us, calling us names or condemning us to hell. Don't take it personally. It has nothing to do with you. It has everything to do with their faith and the shock of having their faith challenged.

The difference between a bulletproof faith and one that cannot handle a challenge is that a bulletproof faith embraces the doubt. It welcomes it, makes it at home, and begins to explore what this fresh doubt means and how it may change, improve, enhance, or have no affect whatsoever on faith. When we embrace doubt as an opportunity for growth and not as an enemy to our faith, we have the ability—and the humility—to say, "If new evidence arises, my faith can adapt without being destroyed."

If you find yourself mired in doubt when someone questions whether you can be gay, lesbian, bisexual, or transgender and remain Christian, don't immediately become defensive or afraid. Instead, explore the source of that doubt. In seminary, when my beliefs were called into question, I had to seriously rethink some of the beliefs that served as the very foundation of my faith. When my Internet antagonist planted seeds of doubt in my mind about whether my take on Scripture might be right or my experiences of God were valid, I began to use my rising doubts to delve deeper into my beliefs. I would examine Scripture, explore the history of the creed or belief that had come into question, and pray and meditate over it. I would talk with others in my community who were knowledgeable about the subject and compare their answers to what I might have read elsewhere or thought of during my prayers and meditations.

Doubts often come bearing gifts. It was through doubting that I discovered some of the greatest theological minds of our times, including Marcus Borg, John Shelby Spong, and Dominic Crossan. Through their writings, I came to see traditional theology in fresh and exciting ways. Their words revitalized my faith and allowed me to believe in and experience God differently—better. I never would have found them unless I had doubted much of orthodox Christianity in seminary.

It was my doubt that actually led me back into the fold of Christian faith. During my frustration in seminary, I came across a book by Leslie Weatherhead called *The Christian Agnostic*. Weatherhead's book gave me the permission I was seeking to put aside the more troubling Christian creeds in a mental box called "awaiting more light" without discarding those creeds and doctrines completely.[3] Doubt has expanded my faith in innumerable ways, leading me to build on and improve the faith I had been given as a child.

While my journey of doubt led me from a conservative faith to a more progressive faith, other GLBT Christians have journeyed with their doubt and have arrived at a more conservative or orthodox faith. A bulletproof faith defies labels of "liberal" or "conservative." The end result, no matter where we fall on the theological spectrum, is a faith that is stronger for our journey with doubt.

What I have discovered is that our doubts should be just as closely scrutinized as our beliefs. Just as faith should not be blind, neither should our doubts. If our faith is to be bulletproof, it must be large enough to embrace doubt and change and grow if that doubt introduces new dimensions to our thinking and believing. Our faith must remain humble enough, though, to admit when it has been holding wrong ideas about God and adapt accordingly.

Karl Barth counseled believers to

> act as those who know. But we must not claim to be those who know. . . . [The power of God's self-revelation] consists in the divine act of majesty in face of which those who really know will always find and confess that they do not know. The attitude of those who know in this power can only be one of the greatest humility. . . . It is just because they can have no doubt as to the liberation which is quite outside their own control that those who are really free to know this matter can never lose a sense of humor in relation to themselves.[4]

Doubt forces us to be humble—not arrogant—in our beliefs, whether we consider ourselves liberal or conservative. Above all, doubt means we must keep a sense of humor about the whole endeavor. When we emerge from struggles with our doubt, our faith is more resilient and does not crumble at the first challenge. We have the assurance of things hoped for, the conviction of things not seen, and the ability to laugh at our own weaknesses.

How to Know Your Faith Is Bulletproof

As you dedicate yourself to developing a bulletproof faith, there are many markers you can use to measure your progress. Welcoming and embracing doubt is one of the most prominent characteristics of a bulletproof faith. Following are some other characteristics. At the core of all of them is the ability to be flexible, gentle with yourself and others, and open to everyone who seeks honest and open dialogue.

A bulletproof faith is confident but never arrogant. When we become bulletproof, we realize that there is a rich tapestry of Christian belief in the world, from the extreme fundamentalist to the extreme liberal. That applies even in our own community. When our faith is strong, it is not threatened by any strain of belief that does not exactly match our own. We have confidence in our experience of God and know God is working with us to bring our authentic self to life in the world.

Those with a bulletproof faith may not agree with the beliefs of others, but instead of focusing on the differences between themselves and others, they are more interested in finding common ground. A bulletproof faith sees those who believe differently simply as other human beings, beloved by God and worthy of our care and concern. No one is truly our enemy. Those who work against us are still God's children, even if their human bigotry has blinded them to God's call to love and work for the welfare of everyone. Even if they are screaming hateful words at us from across busy highways or during church dedications or pride parades, we are impervious to their words. Instead, we see the hurting hearts behind the words. Our concern is not for the differences that divide us but the commonality as God's beloved children that will ultimately unite us.

When we are bulletproof, we have a defense ready, but we are not defensive. We understand that we never need anyone else's approval for our faith because our justification comes from God, not from humans. We understand that all people are on a unique journey with God and that no one can dictate what our faith should look like. So we're never quick to "put up our dukes" when challenges come. Instead, we face any challenge with calm assurance. However, when we are truly called to defend the hope that is within us, we have an answer ready, but we are also prepared to follow Xena's advice and run away. Avoiding pointless arguments is never a defeat. It is simply a good form of self-defense to keep from becoming frustrated or discouraged. We are most persuasive when we simply live our lives as loving, compassionate children of God who seek to serve others in the world. Our sexual orientation or gender identity is truly a small part of our lives. Those who see us at work in the world should always see Christ shining through us first and foremost.

A bulletproof faith is always seeking ways to serve others, even those who work against us. We are not self-absorbed, worrying only about ourselves and our well-being. Instead, when we are bulletproof, we are looking outward, seeking ways to serve others who may be in need. True service does not consider whether the one in need is "worthy." Instead, all we need to know is that another human being is suffering. We must never judge another person as unworthy of our love or our help. All are worthy because all are created and loved by God. We must put aside our own feelings, our own prejudice and bigotry, and get on with the business of loving others as God has loved us, regardless of who they are.

A bulletproof faith spends a lot of time in prayer and meditation. This helps us heal any hatred, prejudice, or bigotry that continues to lurk within our own heart. These are the buttons that get pushed whenever someone challenges our faith, utters hurtful words, or seeks to pass laws against our very lives. These are the buttons that debilitate us, that punch holes in our bulletproof faith and allow feelings of worthlessness, resentment, anger, or hatred to enter our hearts.

We should spend plenty of time working on our heart—reclaiming that authentic self in daily prayer and meditation. When we go inside, it should always be to reconnect with God and strengthen our relationship with God so that we can be more effective servants in the world. If our turning inward leads to self-absorption and a reticence to work in the world, then we know our inner life is making us selfish, and we need to readjust. We must always be careful to cultivate a heart of compassion and love, not just for ourselves, but for all the hurting and suffering people in the world.

A bulletproof faith knows its Bible. I have argued in-depth for trusting our experience of God, but we should not commit the fundamentalist error in reverse and toss Scripture, tradition, and reason out the window. Instead, we must constantly be studying the Bible, digesting the Word, and seeking to learn all we can about the Bible and its history. When we know our Bible well, no one can use it against us a weapon. When people announce, "The Bible says . . . ," we'll know enough to check their assertions. We'll be ready with a gentle and reverent response, and we won't let someone else's opinion about the Bible and what it says put us off balance or undermine our trust in our own experiences of God. (The Recommended Reading section at the back of this book lists works that are particularly useful for anyone who wishes to achieve a deeper understanding and knowledge of the Bible.)

A bulletproof faith is joyful. It can't help but be, because it understands that God created us as we are because God thought we might enjoy living this life. That doesn't mean that every day will be happy and problem-free, but it does mean that we have access to the peace that can pass all understanding. God is the source of our joy, even in tough times. Our faith in God and our past experiences of God give us a solid foundation of joy that we can access even when the clouds roll into our lives. Spend time in prayer and meditation daily, and reconnect to the joy and peace that God promises us when we have faith.

A *bulletproof faith is constantly grateful.* It is grateful for everything in life, the good, the bad, and the ugly. When I was a child, my mother would repeat a phrase to me every time I received something, whether it was something I wanted or not. She would look me in the eye and ask, "What do you say?" I can tell you from harsh experience that the correct answer was not "It's about time! What took you so long?" No, the correct answer was "Thank you." That was the right answer, even if you didn't want to say it. Believe me, there were times when I gritted my teeth and said, "Thank you," even if what I had received were beets or carrots or anything less than what I had asked for or wanted.

There are times that we must grit our teeth and say, "Thank you." In retrospect, though, some of the terrible things that have happened in our lives have turned out to be the best because they have made us stronger and helped us develop a bulletproof faith. When I was in the midst of my battle with my Internet antagonist, it was impossible for me to give thanks for him. I had to say it through gritted teeth. But it was our encounters that strengthened my faith and helped me become bulletproof. Now I can genuinely say that I am thankful for him and for every other "enemy" who challenges, stretches, and strengthens my faith.

In Luke 17:11–19, Jesus heals ten lepers, but only one would make my mother proud. The Samaritan leper—or now, ex-leper—came back to Jesus to thank him. His distinction as a Samaritan is important because it means that even before he had leprosy, he was an outcast. John 4:9 tells us that Jews had no dealings at all with Samaritans. You'll remember it was a Samaritan woman that Jesus speaks with at the well. It was scandalous for a Jew to speak to a Samaritan, even more scandalous than a man speaking to woman. The Samaritans were as hated by the respectable religious people of Jesus' day as gay, lesbian, bisexual, and transgender people are hated by some of the respectable religious folks of our day.

I imagine all of those lepers going through deep depressions, being sick and outcast, and reduced to begging to survive. It's sad just to describe their situation. But only one of them—the one who had been doubly excluded and who had the most to be depressed about—could still feel gratitude and the urgent need to go back to Jesus and express it.

Remember, after his healing, the ex-leper was still a Samaritan. He may no longer be a leper, but he's still an outcast. He's still looked down on by "respectable" society. But thanks to Jesus, his faith is made bulletproof because he is grateful regardless of his condition or social status.

The apostle Paul tells us in 1 Thessalonians 5:18 to give thanks in all circumstances. For those looking for a loophole, give it up. When Paul says "all circumstances," that's what he means. Even when life is terrible, we're expected to give thanks. We must count our blessings. If we don't give thanks, even in the darkest times of our lives, we will most certainly neglect to give thanks during the good times. If we are not constantly grateful for our lives, then just like those nine lepers, we'll take our healing for granted.

Paul's advice to the Thessalonians echoes the prophet Jeremiah's advice to the Jewish exiles in Babylon in Jeremiah 29:4–7. He tells them to settle in. They're not getting out of exile anytime soon, so they need to make the best of it. Build houses, get married, have kids. This is your life right now, so you might as well quite your bellyaching about being in exile and get on with your life.

When our lives get bad, it's like being in exile. We're far away from the homey feelings that make us happy. We're out of our comfort zone. We're in a strange and foreign land, held captive by emotions that will not let us go. It is in those times that we need to heed Jeremiah's advice. Settle in, because the only moment you have is right now. Yesterday is gone, and tomorrow isn't here yet. Get comfortable, set up housekeeping, and make this misery your home, because you will never see your way out of discomfort until you can be present in it now. You cannot map a better future until you know where you are now. Give thanks for being here right now—despite all the despair and hopelessness you may feel. Settle in. Enjoy the feel of this book in your hands. Enjoy your breath. Enjoy your beating heart. Enjoy the blood flowing through your veins. Take a deep breath. Be here now.

What do you say? "Thank you."

Finally, a bulletproof faith is forgiving. When our faith is bulletproof, our hearts are large, inviting in even those who disagree with us. Because of our compassion for others, we find that as our faith grows, we become quicker to forgive those who have harmed us. Forgiveness does not mean that we continue to allow people to hurt us, but it does mean that we let go of our hurt over a situation and move on.

More often than not, forgiveness is for ourselves more than for the offenders. If we continue to hold grudges against people for things they have said or done, we continue to foster those ill feelings—and that harms us more than it harm others. My anger over statements made by fundamentalist Christian leaders or the actions of legislators passing laws against same-gender marriage does them no harm. They don't suffer because of my anger. I am the only one who suffers. I am the one who has to deal with feelings of anger and frustration. For my own peace of mind, I must forgive them—seventy times seven if that's what it takes.

Emmet Fox wrote in *The Sermon on the Mount* that by not forgiving, we "are tied to the thing [we] hate. The person perhaps in the whole world whom you most dislike is the very one to whom you are attaching yourself by a hook that is stronger than steel. Is this what you wish?"[5] By not forgiving those who have harmed us, we forever tie ourselves to them—the persons or things that cause us the greatest discomfort. If we want to free ourselves from people who have caused us harm, our only choice is to forgive them.

Elke Kennedy, a mother in Greenville, South Carolina, knows this all too well. Her twenty-year-old son, Sean, died May 16, 2007, after being attacked and beaten outside a Greenville bar. His head hit the pavement so hard that his brain separated from his brain stem. The man who attacked Sean left a message on the phone of one of Sean's friends saying, "You tell your faggot friend that when he wakes up, he owes me $500 for my broken hand." Since there are no hate crime laws in South Carolina and federal hate crime legislation does not include sexual orientation, Sean's killer faces only a maximum five-year sentence for involuntary manslaughter.

Sean's mother has become an activist in the wake of Sean's death. She began a foundation called Sean's Last Wish dedicated to enacting hate crimes laws not just in South Carolina but at the federal level. I met Mrs. Kennedy at a candlelight vigil held for her son in Columbia, South Carolina, in the months following his death. She is a compassionate, warm, caring, and hurting woman. She keenly feels the absence of her son even as she has found new community among Sean's friends and the total strangers who have gathered around her.

I can't imagine forgiving someone who killed a person as dear as a child. My partner's son is as dear to me as if he were my own. I know that if someone killed him, my partner, or even my beloved cat, I would struggle mightily with the idea of forgiveness. Holding a grudge, fostering hatred for the person who took the life of one so precious to me, would be my natural instinct, but refusing to forgive does nothing to the person who has harmed us. Instead it tears *us* up inside. It can literally destroy our lives.

Standing on the steps of the state capitol building in Columbia, I urged the crowd to seek forgiveness for the man who took Sean's life:

> We cannot end hate crimes until we, ourselves, are willing to give up our own thoughts of violence. We cannot end hate crimes until we, ourselves, give up the idea of retribution. We cannot end hate crimes until we, ourselves, love mercy. We cannot end hate crimes until we, ourselves, stop looking at those who oppose us as our enemies. The legislators in this building are not our enemies. The people of South Carolina are not our enemies. The men who killed Matthew Shepard are not our enemies. The man who killed Sean Kennedy is not our enemy.
>
> They are all human beings, struggling with powers and forces that tell them it's OK to hate, struggling with powers and forces that tell them it's OK to do violence against those who are different. They are people who cannot give up the violence within themselves. They feel threatened, and they lash out in physical or legislative violence. Do not return their hatred with hatred. Instead, return mercy for hatred.
>
> Justice fulfills our need for retribution, but mercy goes beyond justice. Mercy understands that we are all connected and that violence to one person means violence against every person. Mercy sees the humanity in every person, no matter how evil [a person's] actions may be. Mercy means we must be reconciled with even those who have done us the greatest harm. Mercy involves forgiveness. Mercy not only transforms us but transforms enemies into friends. Let us have mercy today.

I was a bit apprehensive about pleading for people to forgive Sean's killer. Forgiveness is a process and something very personal. I was hoping that Mrs. Kennedy had not been offended, but after my speech, she hugged me and said she understood that she must forgive the man who killed her son. She simply wasn't ready to do that yet, but she thanked me for reminding her that she must do so to truly move on. I hope that Mrs. Kennedy and her family will one day find it in their hearts to forgive.

I vividly remember watching a documentary on the death penalty featuring the family of a victim. As they toured the death chamber, the mother of the victim lovingly stroked the gurney where the killer would receive the lethal injections. She talked of her hatred for this man. Her anger was palpable. Later, as they drove to the jail to witness the execution, they became stuck in traffic. The family was frantic, pleading with other drivers and road crews to let them through. Watching them work to move cars and concrete barriers out of their way so that they would not miss their chance to satisfy their blood-lust for the death of this man was breathtaking. Their inability to forgive had made them anxious, angry, mean people. This is what happens when we tie ourselves to the things we hate by failing to forgive. The members of this family needed to forgive the killer not for the killer's sake but for their own sanity. It was clear that their lack of forgiveness was driving them crazy.

Although Mrs. Kennedy may find the strength to forgive her son's killer and break the tie of hatred that binds them together now, I doubt that she will ever reach a point of *liking* the man who took her son. The good news is, we don't have to like those who offend us, but we are commanded to love them. Fox says that love must mean "a vivid sense of impersonal good will."[6]

We must extend that "impersonal good will" to anyone who has offended us—be it protesters, well-meaning preachers, family members, or fundamentalist Christian leaders. We must forgive them for the ill will and horrible lies they spread with impunity about the GLBT community. That doesn't mean we stop working to educate them that what they say and do is harmful and staggeringly unchristian, but we must maintain that "vivid sense of impersonal good will" or else we are not loving as God commands.

Some of us are not yet prepared to go that far in our forgiveness. We can't seem to bring ourselves to forgive people who persecute us, let alone begin to think with anything resembling "good will" toward those who killed Sean Kennedy, Matthew Shepard, and other gays, lesbians, bisexuals, or transgender persons for sport. Fox offers sound advice in this instance. Instead of specifically thinking of how to forgive these individuals, we can start by practicing "general forgiveness."

"When you say your daily prayers, issue a general amnesty, forgiving everyone who may have injured you in any way, and on no account particularize. Simply say: 'I freely forgive everyone.' Then in the course of the day, should the thought of grievance or resentment come up, bless the offender briefly and dismiss the thought."[7]

Fox predicts that you can clear resentment and condemnation out of your life with nothing more elaborate than this general practice of across-the-board forgiveness.

Spiritual Survival Tips

1. Embrace your doubt, and be eager to learn what it has to teach you. Working with and through your doubt will always leave your faith stronger than before.

2. Act as though you know, but never be afraid to explore your doubt and revise your beliefs if you feel so led. Always keep your sense of humor.

3. Be confident in your faith, but never be arrogant. Just as our opponents do not have all the answers, we don't either. Remain humble in your faith.

4. Have a gentle and reverent response ready when your faith is questioned or openly attacked. Know your Bible so that you can answer from Scripture, but rely mainly on your

personal experience of God, and never let anyone belittle or rob you of that experience.

5. Seek to serve others. Everyone is worthy of our love and help.

6. Spend time in prayer and meditation to strengthen your relationship with God.

7. Live joyfully and gratefully. God has created us all good, and that is something we should celebrate daily.

8. Forgive those who have harmed you. Do not forgive for them but for yourself so that you can separate yourself from situations and emotions that damage your faith and prevent you from living joyfully and gratefully.

9

"NO WEAPON SHALL PROSPER"

No weapon that is fashioned against you shall
prosper, and you shall confute every tongue that
rises against you in judgment.

—*Isaiah 54:17*

I once saw a popular television evangelist give a sermon on handling criticism. It was a very positive, upbeat sermon about deflecting the everyday discouragements that we face from friends, family, coworkers, and even strangers. In the midst of his sermon he quoted Isaiah 54:17.

My first thought was "Yeah! You tell 'em!" My next thought was, "Wow, he really took that passage out of context." And he did, quite badly. The author of Isaiah at this point is addressing a nation in exile. He is speaking to a group of people who have lost everything—their homes, their families, their identities. They are oppressed by those who have conquered them—disrespected, marginalized, and hated. The words that the prophet speaks to them aren't intended to help them get through the day when someone tells them their hair looks terrible. These are words spoken to a broken and despondent people. These are words spoken to people who hold little hope of ever being part of "acceptable" society. These are words spoken to people who know persecution as intimately as they know themselves. These are words spoken to people in deep pain and anguish. These are words of hope and healing—words intended to lift their spirits and reassure them that God is still alive and working on their behalf.

These are the words we are desperate to hear from our Creator. Gay, lesbian, bisexual, and transgender people are in exile—cast out from our homes, our churches, our jobs, and our society. We are ostracized and oppressed by dogma, tradition, and legislation. We are a wounded and outcast people, desperate for a word of hope from the one who loves us most.

Earlier in the chapter, the prophet promises the people that they will be established in righteousness: "You shall be far from oppression, for you shall not fear; and from terror for it shall not come near you. If anyone stirs up strife, it is not from me; whoever stirs up strife with you shall fall because of you" (Isaiah 54:14–15).

This is God's promise to us as GLBT Christians. We will one day be established in righteousness—church doors will fling wide, pulpits will be opened, leadership will be freely given. Likewise, society's doors will fling wide, granting us full equality in marriage, employment, and social status. No weapon formed against us will prevent full equality from coming to pass. God does not promise an easy ride, however. There will be those who stir strife—we've all encountered them. The good news is that they are not emissaries from God, and their objections will fall by the wayside. The louder their voices, the more their desperation shows. We are a people in exile, but God is working to free us from our bondage. Our task is to pray and to work—to develop a bulletproof faith that never fails, even in the darkest times.

Hurled Insults

The prominent features of every gay pride event I have attended are antigay protesters. They show up with their signs (sometimes their bullhorns) and loudly proclaim that gay, lesbian, bisexual, and transgender people are an abomination before God and doomed to hell. The protesters are so ubiquitous that I hardly notice them anymore. They're as expected as a rainbow flag. I always limit any interaction with them to a wave or a verse of "Jesus Loves Me." I don't listen to anything they say. Like the protester at my church, their words, like bullets, bounce off me.

That's not everyone's experience of the protesters, however. After one pride march, a congregation member stood during prayer time and talked about how the words of the protesters had cut to his heart. Not in the way the protesters had intended, though. Their words of condemnation had not convinced him God desired for him to no longer be gay. Instead, the words cut because he said he was tired of being told to simply ignore them or pray for them. He believed there had to be some consequences for their words of hatred somewhere. He had found his answer in Nehemiah.

Here is a man who had his critics. His story begins when the Jews returned to Judah after Babylonian captivity. Their city has been destroyed by the Babylonians. The wall around the city had been torn down, leaving them defenseless to attack. Nehemiah was the cupbearer for the Persian king Artaxerxes, who granted him a leave of absence to return to the city to help rebuild the wall.

Not everyone wanted a wall rebuilt around the city. The people around Judah, namely Sanballat, the governor of Samaria, and Tobiah, an Ammonite who may have been part of the government in Ammon, were hostile and determined to stop the project. They used several tactics to try to foil Nehemiah's plan.

First they ridiculed the Judeans, calling them "feeble." They called the Judean wall weak and joked that it would fall if even a fox went up the side (Nehemiah 4:2–3). It was in Nehemiah's response in verses 4–5 that our congregant found comfort: "Hear, O our God, for we are despised; turn their taunt back on their own heads, and give them over as plunder in a land of captivity. Do not cover their guilt, and do not let their sin be blotted out from your sight; for they have hurled insults in the face of the builders."

It helped him to know that God will not forget the words of hatred that these protesters had spoken. It helped him to know that the verbal rocks hurled at the GLBT marchers hurt God's ears and cut God to the quick as well. It was Nehemiah's prayer for those who taunted him and worked against him to encounter the same treatment and be treated as they treated others. If we find it difficult to pray for the well-being of those who work against us, Nehemiah's prayer is a great model to follow. Let us take comfort in knowing that God hears the taunts and slurs hurled at us, and God won't forget them. It's a good thing to remember when we want to return insult for insult. God hears us, too, when we abuse another person. That's all the more reason to connect with your authentic self and make all of your responses gentle and reverent.

Refuse to Be Shaken

That's not the only lesson we need to learn from Nehemiah. Despite the taunts of his enemies, he kept his eye on his goal. He kept working, no matter what his enemies said or did. Nehemiah's enemies went to great lengths to stop the wall's repair, including a tactic GLBT people know very well: they told lies about the Judeans. They reported to the surrounding nations that Nehemiah meant to become king and lead the Jews in rebellion (Nehemiah 6:6–9). They even plotted to attack the city and kill Nehemiah, but nothing they did stopped the rebuilding of the wall.

At one point, two of Nehemiah's enemies asked for a meeting. They told Nehemiah, "come and let us meet together." It seemed like a reasonable request. However, Nehemiah knew their hearts. He said, "They intended to do me harm. And I sent a messenger to them saying, 'I am doing a great work and I cannot come down. Why should the work stop while I leave it and come down to you?'" (Nehemiah 6:2–3).

Those who condemn GLBT people have resorted to every one of the tactics used against Nehemiah. They have ridiculed us, saying, "You can't be gay and still be Christian!" The protester at my church ridiculed me by calling me a false prophet. We're ridiculed as "fags," "sissies," "pansies," "dykes," "she-males," or "he-women."

Our critics constantly tell lies about us. They say we can "change" if we enter reparative therapy programs. They say we are incapable of forming loving, committed relationships and are driven by lust. They paint us as a community that values only partying and wild sex. They tout "research" (studies discredited by the American Psychological Association and others) that claims that gay men get more diseases and die earlier than other men. They lie about the causes of homosexuality, denying any genetic evidence and focusing instead on an absent father or an overbearing mother. They say it is impossible for us to be accepted by God until we change. We must not let their lies and taunts deter us from growing our relationship with God. We must not let critics convince us to commit spiritual suicide and stop the important work we are doing—claiming our authentic selves and creating equality in the church and society for GLBT people. We must be like Nehemiah—show them no mercy and call them on their lies. We must say to our critics what Nehemiah said to his in Nehemiah 6:8: "No such things as you say have been done, for you are inventing them out of your own mind."

The critics, however, do not stop at ridicule and lies. Just like Nehemiah's critics, they often threaten—or even carry out—acts of violence against us. I've been threatened many times, and I'm sure there are even some who would attack and kill me if they could. There are those who have already encountered the violent side of our enemies, enduring physical attacks or paying with their lives. The threat of violence against our community is real. We should never forget that—but it still should not be enough to bring us down from the wall.

Our critics use all these tactics to distract us. Nehemiah wrote of his critics in Nehemiah 6:9, "They all wanted to frighten us, thinking, 'Their hands will drop from the work, and it will not be done.'" No matter what our critics say, do, or threaten to do, we must always resist and give them Nehemiah's answer: "I am doing a great work and I cannot come down."

Nehemiah overcame his enemies using two weapons: prayer and self-defense. When his people were threatened, they prayed intently to God for protection, but they didn't stop there. They put armed guards along the wall to keep their enemies at bay. We must do the same. We must develop a regular practice of prayer, using the Jesus Prayer or other methods. We must have a strong prayer life so that we can maintain that connection to our authentic, God-infused self. We can't stop there, though. We have to practice the art of spiritual self-defense. We must put armed guards around the wall of our heart. Those guards are armed with God's grace and love, which will repel any attack and make us bulletproof.

When you feel under assault, when it feels like the enemies are closing in and you want to give up your faith, remember these words from Kathleen Norris in *Amazing Grace*: "I refuse to be shaken from the fold. It's my God, too, my Bible, my church, my faith, it chose me. But it does not make me 'chosen' in a way that would exclude others. I hope it makes me eager to recognize the good, and the holy, wherever I encounter it."[1]

Here we stand, a part of God's family, whether our enemies like it or not. No matter how severe the attacks that we may face, we must refuse to be shaken from God's fold. We belong here. We are welcome here. We are expected to be here. We are here to do a great work.

Spiritual Survival Tips

1. Do not be afraid of critics when they ridicule you, lie about you, or threaten you. Remember, God has promised that no weapon made against us will prosper. God has promised salvation for all who trust.

2. Use the two most effective weapons you have: prayer and spiritual self-defense. Practice both daily.

3. Know that God will not forget the insults and lies spread by our critics. Our job is to continue working on our relationship with God and for the equality of GLBT people in church and society.

4. Be eager to recognize "the good, and the holy," wherever you encounter it.

5. Rely on God's love and grace, and refuse to be shaken from the fold. God has chosen you and loves you beyond measure.

6. Be bulletproof.

SPIRITUAL SURVIVAL EXERCISE: IS THAT YOUR FINAL ANSWER?

Now that you have completed the book, let's go back to the first chapter and read over your answer to that e-mail I had asked you to jot down. Here is the e-mail again:

> As a Christian, God tells me not to judge others. I love the sinners and hate the sin. God did NOT make you gay. These are lies from the enemy, straight from the pit of hell. You are SO going straight to Hell, you ignorant, misguided, perverted misfit! Not only for choosing this abomination of a lifestyle, but for trying to promote it through the very book it flies in the face of. You make me and God want to vomit! AIDS *is* a cure!

It's still not an easy e-mail to read, even after all we've learned. Take the time now to reflect on your earlier answer to this e-mail. What buttons got pressed for you? What emotions came up as your read the e-mail? What words or phrases triggered feelings of anger, fear, or even hatred toward the letter writer?

Reread your answer carefully, picking out areas where your faith may be in need of strengthening.

Now take a moment to reflect on the e-mail in light of what you've read in this book. Would your responses be different? If so, take the time to write them out now.

If your responses have changed, why? What changed? What prompted the change? Is your focus moving away from how you feel about the letter to what prompted the person to write it in the first place? Are you beginning to see God in the letter writer? Are you beginning to question the pain behind the letter writer's words? Are you no longer taking the letter writer's accusations personally? If so, you may well be on your way to a bulletproof faith.

If you are still struggling with how to reply to this e-mail—or debating whether you need to reply at all—take heart. A bulletproof faith does not form overnight. Read the book again, taking note of the areas that seem difficult for you, and focus your work there. Over time, you'll begin to feel your faith grow stronger. You'll know that it's more important to be happy than it is to prove yourself right to people who oppose us.

When I read e-mails like this now, my heart breaks. Years earlier, I would have become immediately angry. Who is this stranger to tell me about my life and my relationship with God? Now I see something different in the e-mail: I see this person's pain. I feel that pain. There is something in this person's life that is so horrible that he or she feels justified in sending hate-filled messages to strangers. The e-mail has nothing to do with me and everything to do with the sender. The sender is the one in pain, the one seeking some reassurance of God's love.

In more than one instance, I have written long, compassionate letters in response to hate mail. More often than not, I receive an even more vitriolic tirade. My responses are not welcome and may actually exacerbate the senders' pain. They cannot hear words of love and compassion from someone they deem so far outside of God's love. I grieve for those people, and I have stopped communicating with them because I don't wish to deepen their pain. Like my brother-in-law, I can't reach them, but I trust that God will one day find someone who can and will.

On rare occasions, however, I get a gracious reply from people who were originally hateful. I have had many e-mail exchanges that have led to the discovery of common ground among the disagreements. By responding in a reverent and gentle way, I have defused many volatile situations and fostered more understanding across the divide.

Among participants who have done the e-mail exercise during my workshops, the consensus has been that Xena has the best advice—run away. Refuse to engage anyone who fires such a vicious opening salvo. Hit "delete" and move on. This is certainly a viable reaction, but I hope that by now you understand that it's not always fruitless to engage our enemies because they offer us so many gifts and often unexpected joy.

Notes

Introduction

1. Kinsey Institute for Sex, Gender, and Reproduction. "Kinsey's Heterosexual-Homosexual Rating Scale." [http://www.kinseyinstitute.org/resources/ak-hhscale.html]. 1948.

2. Dean H. Hamer. "Genetics and Male Sexual Orientation." *Science*, Aug. 6, 1999, p. 803a. Hamer notes: "Sexual orientation is a complex trait that is probably shaped by many different factors including multiple genes [and] biological, environmental, and sociological influences."

3. The word *homophobia* was used by the psychologist George Weinberg in his 1972 book *Society and the Healthy Homosexual*. He defines homophobia as "a phobia about homosexuals. . . . It was a fear of homosexuals which seemed to be associated with a fear of contagion, a fear of reducing the things one fought for—home and family. It was a religious fear and it had led to great brutality as fear always does." Cited in Gregory M. Herek, "Beyond 'Homophobia': Thinking About Sexual Prejudice and Stigma in the Twenty-First Century." *Sexuality Research and Social Policy*, 2004, *1*(2), 2–24. [http://caliber.ucpress.net/doi/abs/10.1525/srsp.2004.1.2.6]. *Internalized homophobia* occurs when gay men or lesbians feel bad about themselves as a result of society's barrage of disapproving messages about homosexuality.

4. G. Remafedi. "Sexual Orientation and Youth Suicide." *Journal of the American Medical Association*, 1999, *282*, 1291.

5. G. Remafedi, J. Farrow, and R. Deisher. "Risk Factors for Attempted Suicide in Gay and Bisexual Youth." *Pediatrics*, 1991, *87*, 869–876.

Chapter One

1. The six most cited Bible verses used against gay and lesbian people are Genesis 19 (the story of Sodom and Gomorrah), Leviticus 18:22 (20:13 echoes the same prohibition of "men lying with men"), Romans 1:26–27, 1 Corinthians 6:9, 1 Timothy 1:9, and Jude 7. Other passages that have been used against gays and lesbians include Deuteronomy 23:17–18, Judges 19, and 1 Kings 14:24 and 15:12. These are called "clobber passages" because gays and lesbians feel like the Bible is being used as a weapon to browbeat them with. For a full accounting of why these passages *do not* condemn homosexuality, visit *Whosoever*'s "Bible and Homosexuality" page at http://www.whosoever.org/bible.

2. Steven Pressfield. *The Legend of Bagger Vance*. New York: Avon Books, 1995, p. 70.

3. Ibid., p. 68.

4. Søren Kierkegaard. *Works of Love*. New York: HarperCollins, 1962, p. 308.

5. Henri J. M. Nouwen. *Life of the Beloved*. New York: Crossroad, 1992, p. 61.

Chapter Two

1. Steven Pressfield. *The War of Art: Break Through the Blocks and Win Your Inner Battles*. New York: Warner Books, 2002, pp. 152–153.

2. Hans J. Hillerbrand. "The Legacy of Martin Luther," ed. Donald K. McKim. Cambridge: Cambridge University Press, 2003. [http://cco.cambridge.org/extract?id=ccol0521816483_CCOL0521816483A018].

3. John Eldredge. *Waking the Dead*. Nashville, Tenn.: Nelson, 2003, p. 78. Eldredge, by the way, is prominent in the antigay religious community. While much of his book is misogynistic and at times antigay, the other material about living life to the fullest is worth reading. Often we avoid the wisdom of our opponents at our own peril. Eldredge has great advice for GLBT people in his book, whether he intended it or not.

4. Ibid., p. 156.

5. "Diamonds." *MSN Online Encyclopedia*. n.d. [http://encarta.msn.com/encyclopedia_761557986/Diamond.html].

6. Ibid.

7. Louis Evely. *That Man Is You*. Mahwah, N.J.: Paulist Press, 1963, p. 128.

8. Ibid., p. 129.

9. Thich Nhat Hahn. *The Heart of the Buddha's Teachings*. New York: Broadway Books, 1998, p. 84.

Spiritual Survival Exercise: Reclaiming Your Authentic Self

1. Tenzin Gyatso. "The Monk in the Lab." *New York Times*, Apr. 26, 2003, sec. A, p. 19.
2. Ibid.
3. Institute of Applied Meditation. "The Origin of Heart Rhythm Meditation." [http://www.appliedmeditation.org/about_iam/origin.shtml]. 2006.
4. Albert S. Rossi. "Saying the Jesus Prayer." *Saint Vladimir's Orthodox Theological Seminary.* [http://www.svots.edu/Faculty/Albert-Rossi/Articles/Saying-the-Jesus-Prayer.html]. n.d.

Chapter Three

1. Alan Jones. *Reimagining Christianity.* Hoboken, N.J.: Wiley, 2005, p. 49.
2. Paul Alan Laughlin. *Remedial Christianity: What Every Believer Should Know About the Faith but Probably Doesn't.* Santa Rosa, Calif.: Polebridge Press, 2000, p. 36.

Chapter Four

1. Marianne Williamson. *A Return to Love: Reflections on the Principles of A Course in Miracles.* New York: HarperCollins, 1992, p. 96.
2. Steven L. Sears (writer). "Dreamworker." *Xena: Warrior Princess*, season 1, episode 3. First broadcast Sept. 18, 1995.
3. Ralph Waldo Emerson. "Self-Reliance." In Carl Bode and Malcolm Cowley (eds.), *The Portable Emerson.* New York: Penguin, 1981, p. 139.
4. Ibid., p. 160.
5. Ralph Waldo Emerson. "The Over Soul." In Bode and Cowley, *The Portable Emerson*, p. 217.
6. Eldredge, *Waking the Dead*, p. 163.
7. John Greenleaf Whittier. "Mary Garvin," stanza 22. 1856.
8. Douglas Wood. *Old Turtle and the Broken Truth.* New York: Scholastic, 2003, p. 35.
9. Martin Luther King Jr. *Strength to Love.* Minneapolis, Minn.: Augsburg Fortress, 1981, p. 52.
10. Adapted from Soulforce. "A Soulforce Credo About My Adversary." [http://www.soulforce.org/article/679]. 2007.

Chapter Five

1. Adapted from Robert N. Minor. *When You're Having a Religious Argument."* Kansas City, Mo.: Fairness Project, p. 7. [http://www.fairnessproject.org]. 2002.

2. Ibid., p. 2.

3. Philip Gulley and James Mulholland. *If Grace Is True.* New York: HarperCollins, 2003, p. 166.

4. Pressfield, *War of Art*, p. 34.

5. Ibid., p. 35.

Chapter Six

1. Pressfield, *Legend of Bagger Vance*, p. 122.

2. Walter Wink. *The Powers That Be.* New York: Random House, 1999, p. 171.

3. Pressfield, *Legend of Bagger Vance*, p. 121.

4. Dotti Berry and Roby Sapp. "Lunch with Pastor Jay . . ." *Gay into Straight America News Update.* [http://www.gayintostraightamerica.com/index.php?page_id=12&newsletter_id=20]. Oct. 31. 2005.

5. Mel White. *Religion Gone Bad: The Hidden Dangers of the Religious Right.* New York: Tarcher/Penguin, 2006, p. 123.

6. Candace Chellew-Hodge. "Don't Write Off the Right: An Interview with Soulforce Founder Mel White." *Whosoever,* Sept.–Oct. 2007. [http://www.whosoever.org/v12i2/white.shtml].

7. Ibid.

8. Eric Elnes. *The Phoenix Affirmations: A New Vision for the Future of Christianity.* San Francisco: Jossey-Bass, 2006.

9. Eric Elnes. *Asphalt Jesus: Finding a New Christian Faith Along the Highways of America.* San Francisco: Jossey-Bass, 2007.

10. Ibid., p. 82.

11. Ibid., p. 99.

Chapter Seven

1. Toby Johnson. "The Cause of Homosexuality According to Jesus." [http://www.tobyjohnson.com/cause.html]. n.d.

Chapter Eight

1. Harry Emerson Fosdick. *A Faith for Tough Times*. New York: HarperCollins, 1952, p. 90.

2. Mother Teresa. *Come Be My Light: The Private Writings of the "Saint of Calcutta,"* ed. Brian Kolodiejchuk. New York: Doubleday, 2007, p. 193.

3. Leslie D. Weatherhead. *The Christian Agnostic*. New York: Abingdon Press, 1965, p. 21.

4. Karl Barth. *The Doctrine of the Word of God,* trans. G. T. Thomson. Edinburgh: Clark, 1936, p. 57.

5. Emmet Fox. *The Sermon on the Mount: The Key to Success in Life*. New York: HarperCollins, 1966, p. 173.

6. Ibid., p. 175.

7. Ibid., p. 176.

Chapter Nine

1. Kathleen Norris. *Amazing Grace*. New York: Riverhead Books, 1998, p. 143.

Recommended Reading

Brentlinger, Rick. *Gay Christian 101: Spiritual Self-Defense for Gay Christians*. Pace, Fla.: Salient Press, 2007.

Buehrens, John A. *Understanding the Bible: An Introduction for Skeptics, Seekers, and Religious Liberals*. Boston: Beacon Press, 2003.

Countryman, L. William. *Dirt, Greed, and Sex: Sexual Ethics in the New Testament and Their Implications for Today*. Minneapolis, Minn.: Augsburg Fortress, 1988.

Countryman, L. William, and Ritley, M. R. *Gifted by Otherness: Gay and Lesbian Christians in the Church*. Harrisburg, Pa.: Morehouse, 2001.

England, Michael E. *The Bible and Homosexuality*. San Francisco: Universal Fellowship of Metropolitan Community Churches, 1986.

Gomes, Peter. *The Good Book: Reading the Bible with Mind and Heart*. New York: Morrow, 1996.

Helminiak, Daniel. *What the Bible Really Says About Homosexuality*. San Francisco: Alamo Square Press, 1994.

Horner, Tom. *Jonathan Loved David: Homosexuality in Biblical Times*. Louisville, Ky.: Westminster/John Knox, 1978.

Johnson, Toby. *Gay Spirituality: The Role of Gay Identity in the Transformation of Human Consciousness*. Maple Shade, N.J.: Lethe Press, 2004.

Jordan, Mark. *The Invention of Sodomy*. Chicago: University of Chicago Press, 1996.

Katz, Jonathan. *The Invention of Heterosexuality*. New York: Dutton, 1996.

McNeill, John J. *The Church and the Homosexual*. Boston: Beacon Press, 1993.

McNeill, John J. *Taking a Chance on God*. Boston: Beacon Press, 1988.

Miner, Jeff, and Connoley, John Tyler. *The Children Are Free: Reexamining the Biblical Evidence on Same-Sex Relationships*. Indianapolis, Ind.: Jesus Metropolitan Community Church, 2002.

Minor, Robert. *Scared Straight: Why It's So Hard to Accept Gay People and Why It's So Hard to Be Human*. Saint Louis, Mo.: Humanity Works, 2001.

Minor, Robert. *When Religion Is an Addiction*. Saint Louis, Mo.: Humanity Works, 2007.

Palmer, Wendy. *The Practice of Freedom: Aikido Principles as a Spiritual Guide*. Berkeley, Calif.: Romdell Press, 2002.

Rogers, Jack. *Jesus, the Bible, and Homosexuality: Explode the Myths, Heal the Church*. Louisville, Ky.: Westminster/John Knox, 2006.

Rudy, Kathy. *Sex and the Church*. Boston: Beacon Press, 1997.

Scanzoni, Letha, and Mollenkott, Virginia Ramey. *Is the Homosexual My Neighbor?* San Francisco: HarperOne, 1978.

Scroggs, Robin. *The New Testament and Homosexuality*. Minneapolis, Minn.: Augsburg Fortress, 1983.

Siker, Jeffrey S. (ed.). *Homosexuality in the Church: Both Sides of the Debate*. Louisville, Ky.: Westminster/John Knox, 1994.

Smith, Denny. *God Did TOO Make Adam and Steve*. Saint Cloud, Minn.: Dennis Smith Training and Development, 2004.

Spong, John Shelby. *Rescuing the Bible from Fundamentalism: A Bishop Rethinks the Meaning of Scripture*. New York: HarperCollins, 1991.

Spong, John Shelby. *The Sins of Scripture: Exposing the Bible's Texts of Hate to Reveal the God of Love*. New York: HarperCollins, 2005.

Truluck, Rembert. *Steps to Recovery from Bible Abuse*. Gaithersburg, Md.: Chi Rho Press, 2000.

Weatherhead, Leslie D. *The Christian Agnostic*. Nashville, Tenn.: Abingdon Press, 1990.

White, Mel. *Stranger at the Gate: To Be Gay and Christian in America*. New York: Simon & Schuster, 1994.

Online Resources

Meditation

Centering Prayer:
http://www.contemplativemind.org/practices/prayer.html

Christian Meditation:
http://christianmeditation.com

Loving-Kindness Meditation:
http://www.contemplativemind.org/practices/loving-kindness.html

Mindfulness Meditation:
http://www.meditationcenter.com/connect/mind.html

World Community for Christian Meditation:
http://www.wccm.org

Bible and Homosexuality

The Bible, Christianity, and Homosexuality, by Justin Cannon:
http://www.truthsetsfree.net/bible.htm

The Christian Bible and the Homosexual, by Dean Worbois:
http://www.postfun.com/pfp/homosexual.html

Comprehensive Bible commentary by Rembert Truluck:
http://www.otkenyer.hu/truluck/six_bible_passages.html

Homosexuality and Christianity from the Cathedral of Hope:
http://www.cathedralofhope.com/homosexuality

Homosexuality and Christianity, by Jeramy Townsley:
http://www.jeramyt.org/gay.html

Homosexuality and the Bible, by Walter Wink:
http://www.bridges-across.org/ba/wink.htm

Homosexuality and the Bible: The Practice of Safe Texts, by Reverend Robert E. Goss:
http://www.geocities.com/~mcc_st_louis/homo.htm

A Letter to Louise, by Bruce Lowe:
http://www.godmademegay.com/Letter.htm

Religious Tolerance.org (very comprehensive site):
http://www.religioustolerance.org/hom_bibl.htm

What the Bible Says—and Doesn't Say—About Homosexuality, by Reverend Mel White:
http://www.soulforce.org/whatthebiblesays.pdf

Whosoever magazine's section on the Bible and homosexuality:
http://www.whosoever.org/bible

The Author

Candace Chellew-Hodge is a recovering Southern Baptist. Born in 1965 as the grand finale of five children to a Southern Baptist minister and his wife, she comes by her need for recovery honestly.

Chellew-Hodge literally grew up in the church, playing with her G.I. Joe dolls and Tonka trucks in the sanctuary aisles. Her family was still shocked when she came out as a lesbian years later, despite the obvious clues.

She gave up her faith at age seventeen, about the same time she entered a career in journalism that would span two and a half decades (including a six-year stint at CNN in Atlanta), but despite the allegations of some conservative pundits, the media were not to blame for making her Godless for a brief few years. Instead, Chellew-Hodge did what so many gay, lesbian, bisexual, and transgender people do—she believed the lie that she couldn't be both a lesbian and a Christian.

She returned to the church in her early twenties, kicking and screaming, at the insistence of her first girlfriend. She describes her first service at a Metropolitan Community Church in Atlanta as "coming home."

Chellew-Hodge entered seminary in 1998, a couple of years after she founded *Whosoever: An Online Magazine for Gay, Lesbian, Bisexual, and Transgender Christians*. The magazine had drawn the attention of many opponents of GLBT equality in church and society, and Chellew-Hodge sought the tools to answer her critics. What she discovered in seminary was a whole new way to approach the question of homosexuality, gender identity, and spirituality and a new way to respond to critics that was a lot less stressful.

Chellew-Hodge graduated from the Candler School of Theology at Emory University in Atlanta in 2002 with a master of theological studies degree. She was ordained in 2003 by Gentle Spirit Christian Church in Atlanta. In July 2004, she became assistant pastor at Garden of Grace United Church of Christ in Columbia, South Carolina (what was then MCC Columbia). In 2007, she was licensed as a United Church of Christ minister and made associate pastor at Garden of Grace. Chellew-Hodge is also a spiritual director, trained through the Episcopal Diocese of Atlanta.

For more information, see http://whosoever.org. A free *Bulletproof Faith* study guide and other resources are available at http://www.bulletproofbook.com.

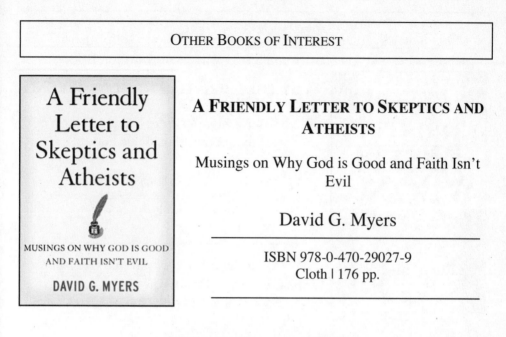

A FRIENDLY LETTER TO SKEPTICS AND ATHEISTS

Musings on Why God is Good and Faith Isn't Evil

David G. Myers

ISBN 978-0-470-29027-9
Cloth I 176 pp.

A response to the new atheists...

A prominent psychologist, writer, and Christian, David Myers uses *A Friendly Letter to Skeptics and Atheists* to respond to critics such as Sam Harris, Richard Dawkins, Christopher Hitchens, and Daniel Dennett. Writing as a respected and well-known scientist with a broad and generous Christian background, Myers acknowledges the faults and failings of religion and the sins committed in its name and presents a well-reasoned case for the many benefits of faith—not just for individuals, but for society at large. He demonstrates why God *is* good, why this is *not* the end of faith, and how we may have many delusions but God is *not* one of them.

"Witty, disarming, engaging, informative, and above all, great fun to read. The best response to the 'New Atheism' to date."

— **Alister McGrath**, Oxford University theologian-biophysicist

DAVID G. MYERS is the John Dirk professor of Psychology at Michigan's Hope College and the author of 15 books as well as articles in dozens of periodicals, from *Scientific American* to *Christianity Today*. He is on the board of the Templeton Foundation, whose mandate is to seek reconciliation between science and religion.

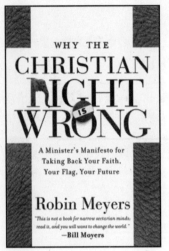

WHY THE CHRISTIAN RIGHT IS WRONG

A Minister's Manifesto for Taking Back Your
Faith, Your Flag, Your Future

Robin Meyers

ISBN 978-0-470-18463-9
Paper | 224 pp.

"This is not a book for narrow sectarian minds; read it, and you will want to change the world." **–Bill Moyers**

"This is a timely warning and a clarion call to the church to recover the Gospel of Jesus Christ and to a great nation to resist the encroachment of the Christian Right and of Christian fascism. Many of us in other parts of the world are praying fervently that these calls will be heeded."
–The Most Reverend Desmond M. Tutu, Archbishop Emeritus

In November 2004, Oklahoma minister Robin Meyers achieved instant fame when the text of his antiwar speech, given at a peace rally at the University of Oklahoma, spread like wildfire in cyberspace. He became a voice crying in the wilderness, a midwestern Christian in the reddest of red states who unapologetically denounced the values of the Christian Right and the Bush Administration and called for a higher standard–one true to the biblical values that conservatives claim to hold.

Building on the themes of his now-famous speech, Meyers claims peace, poverty, and the environment, among others, as religious concerns, and points out how the values of the Christian Right and the Bush administration conflict with the gospel of Christ. Indignant without being self-righteous, this book offers positive, practical advice on resistance and advocacy.

ROBIN MEYERS, a nationally known minister and peace activist, syndicated columnist, and award-winning commentator, is a professor of rhetoric at Oklahoma City University.

LET YOUR LIFE SPEAK

Listening for the Voice of Vocation

Parker J. Palmer

ISBN 978-0-7879-4735-4
Hardcover I 128 pp.

Discover your path in life

Let Your Life Speak is an insightful and moving meditation on finding one's true calling. The book's title is a time-honored Quaker admonition, usually taken to mean "Let the highest truths and values guide everything you do." But Palmer reinterprets those words, drawing on his own search for selfhood. "Before you tell your life what you intend to do with it," he writes, "listen for what it intends to do with you. Before you tell your life what truths and values you have decided to live up to, let your life tell you what truths you embody, what values you represent." Sharing stories of frailty and strength, of darkness and light, Palmer will show you that vocation is not a goal to be achieved but a gift to be received.

"Clear, vital, honest. . . . Immerse yourself in the wisdom of these pages and allow it to carry you toward a more attentive relationship with your deeper, truer self."
— **John S. Mogabgab**, editor, *Weavings* Journal

PARKER J. PALMER, writer, teacher, and activist, is senior associate of the American Association for Higher Education and senior advisor to the Fetzer Institute. In 1998, he was named one of the thirty most influential senior leaders in higher education. Author of such widely praised books as *The Courage to Teach* and *The Promise of Paradox*, he holds a Ph.D. from the University of California at Berkeley. He is a member of the Religious Society of Friends (Quaker) and lives in Madison, Wisconsin.